ELEMENTS OF SOCIAL AND POLITICAL PHILOSOPHY

MELBOURNE INTERNATIONAL PHILOSOPHY SERIES

VOLUME 2

ELEMENTS OF SOCIAL AND POLITICAL PHILOSOPHY

J. T. J. SRZEDNICKI

Communications to be addressed to the Editor, c/o Philosophy Department, University of Melbourne, Parkville, 3052, Victoria, Australia.

ELEMENTS OF SOCIAL AND POLITICAL PHILOSOPHY

by

J. T. J. SRZEDNICKI

MARTINUS NIJHOFF – THE HAGUE – 1976

ISBN 90 247 1744 2

PRINTED IN THE NETHERLANDS

TABLE OF CONTENTS

INTRODUCTION

The general purpose of this book differs from those of most of the works found traditionally in the field of political philosophy.

Firstly, the present approach is in no way prescriptive or normative, as the interest centres on explication rather than an evaluative assessment of this, that or another type of arrangement, or act.

It will be clear that I am in complete disagreement with Gewirth[1] when he claims that "The central concern of political philosophy is the moral evaluation of political power." It seems obvious that the *understanding* of political and social forms of life, and *a fortiori* of political power, must come before its evaluation. This cannot be provided by moral assessment alone. Thus an analytical or explicative approach which promotes such understanding must come first, and must be the "central concern" of the appropriate philosophical discipline. This is not to say that moral assessment is illegitimate, nor even that it cannot be one of the concerns of political philosophy, but it is to deny that it can be central, even though it might be somebody's central interest. To the extent to which this book is successful it will provide an argument in my favour – if the job can be done, obviously it is of primary importance. But we should not assume that it cannot be done unless we can show that there is no separate sphere of political and/or social phenomena. To do this would again require understanding of the problems as such rather than their moral assessment, and it would be a job prior to such assessment. Thus Gewirth's view seems quite implausible.

Besides being explicatory, the method adopted here is conceptual. It concentrates on the analysis of what appear to be the central concepts and terms in the field. Since there is by no means an accepted or obvious list of such terms, one of the primary tasks of the book, particularly of its first part, is to try to establish what they are.

The list here arrived at is not the only one possible, but the selected

[1] A. Gewirth (ed.), *Political Philosophy*, Macmillan, 1965, Introduction, p. 1 ff.

terms are intuitive, functionally related, and such that with extension and additions they could be used to discuss any social political issue. The terms found in ordinary parlance could not be left entirely in their everyday form, for, in this field above all, vagueness and equivocation haunt ordinary language. The reason is not far to seek – social and political actions are characteristically public. Here it is impossible to emulate the hypocrite who, say, in the area of sexual morality, preaches one thing and secretly does another. In public action it is imperative that one should at least appear to be doing what one preaches. The commonest way out consists in twisting the words in order to change their meaning while retaining their emotional force. Thus, in this way at least, the terminology becomes a tool of deception. But it is a tool in very many other ways as well. In the field of social engineering it is imperative to obtain agreement and cooperation, It is also less important to agree on the precise reasons and their correctness, than on actual working arrangements. Thus throughout the field language in general, and the proper socio-political jargon in particular, are prime instruments *directly* employed in action. Consequently the jargon adapts to particular needs and styles, and overall linguistic precision, as well as clarity of expression, are lost. Words become theory-culture-ideology orientated, and it begins to be difficult to state with objective transparency what are the achievements of others as well as our own shortcomings. All this is an obvious impediment for a researcher who needs theory-invariant terminology to be able to state, let alone handle, his problems. To obtain one is one of the main aims of this book.

I have generally taken a common word, as free as possible from scars acquired in political practice, and have tightened it up, i.e. I provide a definition, and keep my use within the limits thus stated. But the definitions are not simply stipulative, they are in addition corrective. Each time an attempt is made to limit the term to what is naturally its basic or core sense, and to sweep away all the paraphernalia detrimental to precision and clarity of expression. The hope is that the finished product will be intuitive, easy to absorb, requiring some adjustment, but not necessitating the learning of a new and strange terminology. The statements made with the help of the terms thus provided should be easily intelligible to any speaker of English, but *for precise discussion* he would need to *bear in mind the limitations imposed by the system.* This type of method is outlined by Quine in *Word and Object.* Quine says: "This construction is paradigmatic of what we are most typically up to when in a philosophical spirit we offer an 'analysis' or 'explication' of some hitherto inadequately formulated 'idea' or expression. We do not claim synonymy. We do not claim to make clear and explicit what the users of the unclear expression had unconsciously meant all along. We do not expose hidden meanings, as the words 'analysis' and 'explication' would suggest: we supply facts. We fix on the particular functions of the unclear expression that make it worthwhile troubling about, and then devise a substitute, clear and couched in terms to our liking, that fills those functions."[2]

One of the main problems is the selection of the basic terms. I have adopted the method of finding them in analysis. That is, I begin by searching for the basic, ground-floor questions in the field, e.g. "What is the nature of communal co-operation?" – it then becomes quite clear that what one is asking about has a natural name in English, i.e. "co-operation", and also reasonably clear in what sense the term applies with respect to our question. This then is taken to be the main sense for our purpose. From then on the argument is developed and terms emerge as questions and problems emerge. Throughout this search I am always concerned with the possible rather than the actual forms of interpersonal intercourse, thus the study is non-empirical and paradigmatic. It is the aim of the method to make contact with the more central and basic of those forms, so, as well as appealing to what might be termed a logical priority of some forms rather than others, some recourse must be made to general empirical intuition. The presentation of the findings could be likened to an exploded drawing, such as are commonly used in gunnery instruction. An attempt is made to build up the terminology in a functional and explanatory order. Terms are, so to say, seen posed for action, their relative order, importance and ramifications exhibited in the order and manner of presentation.

Thus the book seeks to be more than just a terminological adventure, for it is hoped that at least some basic concepts, their relations and the basic distinctions, will be found and understood in the process. The highest ambition consists in the wish that the terminological advantage should be bound up with improved understanding, and some clarification of difficulties.

Clearly the enterprise is theoretical. In this respect I am in general agreement with Peter Winch[3] who claims: "In dealing with questions

[2] W. V. O. Quine, *Word and Object*, MIT Press, 1960, p. 258–259.

[3] P. Winch, *The Idea of a Social Science and its Relation to Philosophy*, Routledge & Kegan Paul, 1958, p. 18 ff.

of this sort there should be no question of waiting to see 'what empirical research will show us,' it is a matter of tracing the implications of the concepts we use. Winch takes his ideas considerably further and there we part company". For instance he chastises Mill for wishing to "observe regularities in the behaviour of its (social institutions) participants and expressing these regularities in the form of generalisations."[4] In other places Winch himself stresses the fact that in *each science* there are prior conceptual matters that arise.[5] There does not seem to be any good reason to deny that appropriate generalisations are possible with respect to a society and its conceptual system, provided the conceptual system is taken into account when they are formed. Indeed if assessment of an alien conceptual apparatus was really impossible Winch could hardly make his point, or argue for it in the way he does. This view leads further to a tenet with which I am in complete disagreement, to wit: that it is impossible in principle to compare really different social systems.

From the purely terminological point of view the main advantages of the system developed in this book lie in the fact that the terms are likely to be both intuitive and functionally related. Its main disadvantage is in the close ties between the terminology that emerges and the research method adopted. It seems that since such a tie, even when its existence is not obvious, would in any case exist, it is better to make its presence explicit.

There are two safeguards against the ills of the situation.

Firstly, the terms are as natural and intuitive as possible, even though precision and clarity must be the main desideratum. Thus the terminology is not only tied to the method, but also to ordinary language – if the selection of terms is theory-bound their character is reasonably theory-invariant. This is a valuable, if not a complete, check.

Secondly, a serious attempt is made to ask the absolutely basic questions first, and to make sure that they are basic, *viz.* such that an answer to these questions in this order is necessary before we can ask any further questions with understanding. To the extent to which this attempt is successful it is possible to claim that the order is objective, or at least as objective as any other, and that this objectivity carries over to the terminology discovered by the analysis. Where the analysis is unsuccessful no such claim can be made, and it would be too much to

[4] *Ibid.*, p. 86, par. 6.
[5] *Ibid.*, *passim*, e.g. p. 84–6, cf. also E. Husserl, "Philosophy as Strict Science."

hope to be able to ensure that the terminology should be more successful than the method that produced it.

One of the main points of this study is to show that political and social philosophy is not basically a normative discipline, that it should be primarily concerned with the concepts appertaining to the logically possible forms of interpersonal intercourse, and it is not primarily concerned with the norms of acceptable behaviour in such situations. This is not to deny that the other type of study is legitimate and philosophical, but perhaps to suggest that it is secondary and applied, and certainly to maintain that the type of study envisaged here is philosophical, basic and necessary.

Partly on merit and partly for economy of space the argument is developed in the form of a system, thus results accepted earlier are to be understood to impose limitations on subsequent discussion. Notably what is said is often open to a much narrower interpretation than it would be if it appeared in, say, an independent article. In at least some places, if such a wider interpretation is placed on the arguments they might not be sufficient, while they are sufficient as they stand. Unfortunately, it would take too much space to make such points explicit throughout the book.

I have tried to meet what appeared to be important objections to the points raised in the course of the argument. Again for reasons of space I could not treat all discernible objections, even if this was permissible from the point of view of transparency.

In writing this book I have received valuable help from many people. I cannot possibly mention them all, though I wish to express my thanks to all. I could not omit to mention Prof. J. Plamenatz of All Souls College, Oxford; Prof. H.J. McCloskey of La Trobe University; Mr. A. Quinton of New College, Oxford; Prof. H.L.A. Hart of University College, Oxford; Prof. H. Wolfson and Mr. G. Weiler of La Trobe University; Prof. T. Kotarbinski, University of Warsaw; Mr. V. Bogdanor of Brasenose College, Oxford; Mr. H. Redner of Monash University; Dr. M. McCloskey and Ms. L.M. Broughton of Melbourne University. All these people have offered valuable criticism, suggestions and encouragement at different stages of the work. I should also express my appreciation of the many valuable points raised by students at Melbourne University who at various times attended my lectures in Political Philosophy.

As I have only accepted those suggestions that appealed to me, I alone am responsible for any faults found in this book.

CHAPTER I

COMMUNITY

The State, the obvious subject of political study, is only the most sophisticated and complex form of communal life. It could not exist in the absence of some community, for it comprises a number of these as well as other structures, institutions, etc.

The first problem then concerns the basis and the nature of a community. There are interpersonal sets that are not communities. The simplest of them being a collection. We can have collections of: stones, ancient rugs, pictures, stamps, bank accounts, manufacturing companies, friends, etc. Most of them are not communities, for instance, a museum is not a community of pictures. What then is missing? Often we have a wrong type of individual, for example, pictures and bank accounts are inanimate. But this is not the point of the distinction, only a symptom. A zoo is not a community of animals, though they are animate. Nor yet will specifying a more likely type of individual provide the answer. Intelligent, civilized people are a prime example of the right type of individual. But take forty such people waiting together for a bus, they are not a community for this reason alone. Yet a collection of less suitable individuals can form a community; savages and conceivably ants live in communities.[1]

Inanimate objects are clearly incapable of the kind of relation that gives rise to a community. What kind of relation then is missing between: people waiting for a bus, ants in a bottle, not organised inmates of a cell, etc.?

To avoid being a merely accidental collection a community must be grounded in a bond that forms between its members and finds expression in what they do, expect, believe, etc. Communities are typically a way of life from the point of view of their members. Besides this, the relations between individuals forming a community must bind the in-

[1] The method adopted in the first part of the first chapter is parallel to that used by Max Weber for a similar purpose in *Basic Concepts of Sociology*, Citadel, 1969.

dividuals to each other without outside help. They should also explain the kind of unity and co-operation that is displayed by the communal organism as such.

Let us then look for the kind of relation that *could* conceivably form the basis of communal life. What is needed is a bond of such a kind that there is nothing *preventing it* becoming a foundation of a community, something that is minimally sufficient for this purpose. If we find a relation that can operate fully and yet fail to create a community type condition, it is insufficient. But to be sufficient it need not create a community, only an interdependence that is recognisably of the kind needed to form a social group. In order to make this clearer let us look for likely cases and candidates. The majority of them will not do. Apart from lack of animation, a heap of stones is not a candidate for a community, yet the relation between stones is significant for their arrangement. They keep each other in place and exert pressure on each other. Clearly if stones were replaced by poets, a community would not come into being.[2] In an avalanche, an unstable arrangement, the stones have a common effect which results from their interaction. Since an avalanche is not a community, the plausible proposal that communities are distinguished by producing effect *qua* communities is clearly insufficient. What is missing?

Quite obviously in such a case, again even if the avalanche consisted of poets not stones, there would be no community, the significant fact consisting in that in such a case there is no purpose in the arrangement – the effect just happens to be what it is. Since this will not do it is necessary to consider a relation that has some point, a situation where the combined effect of all the individuals thus related serves some purpose. Perhaps this stricter requirement will provide us with the sought after criterion? Will it be enough to handcuff people in a deliberate pattern, or harness the oxen? This question emphasises two points. *Firstly*, the communal bond typically leaves the individuals as separate as ever, they are independent though related, capable of individual actions, and yet it is precisely in this area that we expect the bond to operate. However it should be noted that by "independent" I mean here merely "able to decide otherwise" or "able to refuse to cooperate." I do not mean to indicate independence in the sense in which an individual is independent provided only that it is safe for him to refuse cooperation with others. Thus an individual is independent in the required sense if

[2] Cf. here H. L. A. Hart, *The Concept of Law*, Oxford, 1961, p. 9: "Mere convergence of behaviour between members . . . may exist . . . and yet there might be no rule *requiring* it," etc.

and only if he can refuse to cooperate even if such a refusal were to mean the ruin of himself or even of everybody concerned.[3]

A group where all communally required action had to be physically enforced could not exist, for who would do the enforcing? This shows that *a bond in independence* is a necessary requirement. It is usually claimed that this happens if rules are internalised, which while true might be regarded as an insufficient explanation. This requirement admits of individual exceptions in practice for a man deprived of his freedom of action by imprisonment, does not cease to be a member of the community which imprisoned him. Having noted this last problem, it is best to leave it aside and proceed.

Secondly, the relations must have point and/or be desirable from the point of view of the individuals forming the community in question, for then and only then is there any real possibility of the arrangement working in its own right. The individuals must see the set-up as worthwhile. Whether this view of theirs is correct and what are the grounds for it is relatively unimportant, and shall not claim our attention at least at present.

To make things clearer, let us think of a colony of bacteria: its members are capable of behaviour, for some activities are initiated by the bacteria themselves. Bacteria, let us assume, are capable of reacting to stimuli, but all the stimuli are so much on a par that no discrimination or assessment of the world around them is possible. Now if the existence of a sufficient number of bacteria in a place creates favourable conditions for others then the bacteria will tend to converge there. This behaviour is conditioned by the presence of the others in the vicinity. Do we have a community?

The individuals in this group do not see the relations between themselves as having a point – they do not see themselves as standing in any relation at all – they simply react to stimuli. Yet the relations *are in fact* desirable from the point of view of individual bacteria. Yet there is no community for the behaviour of any of the bacteria is in no way directly and even more importantly *qua* behaviour, responsible for the behaviour of any other. Each of the bacteria reacts to its environment and each of the bacteria has its effects on its environment. It is by those indirect means that a semblance of concerted action is created. Significantly it would make no difference whatever to a given bacillus if the

[3] The need for this specific qualification was brought to my notice by a point raised by Mr. E. Hübel in his 1972 examination paper.

conditions were due to something else, even to absence of other bacilli. Members of a community however must stand in some sort of more direct relation to each other; this relation must be "in principle" sufficient to enable all the members of the community to act towards one common end. It is the hallmark of a community that while composed of individuals it *can* act as a single unit. This capability must derive from the direct influence the individuals have on each other *qua* individuals. Otherwise the effect, though fortunate, and in some cases assured, is not designed but is a happy chance. A community consists precisely in this, that its members deliberately co-operate. In practice it might be difficult to decide (e.g. ants) whether there is co-operation or happy chance, but since this is not a conceptual difficulty it need not detain us here.

In a flock of sheep or a shoal of fish individuals act as a result of actions of others, and *in order* to concert with their action, they follow each other and stay together, so the above requirement seems to be satisfied, yet a flock is hardly a community. What then is missing at this stage?

Possibly for a community concerted behaviour must mean that it is the *purpose* of the members of a community to behave in a concerted or common fashion, and the sheep or the fish do not behave in that way. Theirs is an instinctive reaction, not a purposive behaviour. While they react directly to the actions of other sheep, these are no more than a privileged stimulus, there is no design, even if there is a desire not to be left behind when the other sheep move away. We have again a natural phenomenon rather than deliberately concerted actions.

Let us ask: How is the having reasons for acting related to having a community and to people being members of a community? It would not be sufficient if the 'members' were capable of having reasons for their actions. For if the reasons were unconnected with the concerted effort, this would not do, clearly it would not help in such a case if the reasons concerned other individuals in the collection, not even if the resultant actions were directed at them.

Other individuals can be treated as conditions for action and a group structure short of community could emerge. Take a pecking order case - the order is determined simply by relative prowess of birds who do not peck at stronger birds but do peck at weaker mates. The resultant structure is neither directed at a common good nor deliberate, as is shown by the fact that reasons need not be present. Clearly if we add reasons and specify that the arrangement rests on reasons we would hardly have a community. In fact a classical case of lack of community, Hobbes' "State of Warre," fits our picture.[4]

The minimal conditions for saying that I might be acting in concert with you exist if your opinions concerning your and my behaviour are my reasons, or at least part of my reason for acting in this way.

It must be added that *A's belief must be B's reason for acting in the way consonant with A's wishes.* Otherwise, A's wish would be merely a condition that B takes into account. As for instance a bully or a tease might be spurred to further devilry by his knowledge of his victim's wish to be left alone. Let us express this requirement by saying that *A's belief or wish must be in a positive way, the reason for B doing this or that.*

The requirement that e.g. your beliefs, expectations, convictions, attitudes or wishes[5] concerning actions on your, mine or somebody's part should be in a positive way my reasons for acting in the specified manner (not necessarily my sole reason) will also avoid the case in which one acts completely independently but is inclined to take *somebody else's good into account.*

Buddhists are kind to insects without inquiring for insect-wishes. A number of individuals bent on altruistic behaviour towards each other could easily exist together, for their kindness would be mutual, but they would not be a community – they could not undertake a common project. Each and every one of them would be still *acting completely independently,* other people would in no way be regarded as *taking part in his action,* but only as part of the conditions in which he acts, as *involved in his aims.* It is for this kind of reason that we cannot be said to co-operate with a sick dog when we tend to it.

This is a crucial point. A community is typically capable of deliberate common action directed towards a common or communal goal. Such capability is the very point of the communal set-up, in this way more can be undertaken, with far more expectation of success. This is the obvious point of co-operation between individuals. *What then is the nature and what is the basis of inter-individual co-operation?* This is an important problem, for the argument up to date shows that communal and perforce social as well as political problems are based on, and cannot be understood properly without, a prior understanding of it. As has been shown, co-operation requires more than kind-heartedness and

[4] T. Hobbes, *Leviathan.*

[5] For the sake of brevity I will henceforth use "wishes" as an abbreviation for some such list, and will take it that action will be consonant with much wishes, unless otherwise specified.

having common effect in mass action. When one person's wishes are regarded by another positively as reasons for acting we have a beginning of it, for in this case, two (or more) individuals can *share the same reason* and thus have the same aim – this is the importance of the abovementioned formula.

Since feelings, reactions, motives are tied to individuals who experience them, they cannot be common to many. But a proposition can be expressed or started on many different occasions and in many different ways, it can be held or believed by many different individuals. The proposition that we should finish painting this room before going home, can be believed by all of us and remain the same, thus if we accept it as a reason for acting it is the same for all of us. It could be objected that this should be sufficient without mentioning the wishes of others, but it is not. If A does x for he accepts proposition p as the reason for x-ing, and does know that B, C, D etc. also believe p and accept it as reason for x-ing, he in no way co-operates with them. Co-operation is to do things together and arises (a) when different individuals share a reason, (b) when they know that they share it and, (c) when the fact that they share it is a positive factor in their actions. The third condition is basically fulfilled if A's knowledge (belief) that B holds proposition p is A's reason for acting in a way such that B would be satisfied in view of the fact that he holds p. For example if p = nudity is offensive, and A's action is to refrain from nudity in B's presence.

As long as one person's reasons are unconnected with wishes of others, he is his own boss absolutely, i.e. only what he decides, his own reasons and motives etc. count for him. It is then entirely up to him what end he pursues and how. Consequently no one else has any reason to count on his continuing with any project, or on his taking any project up. It would not be necessary for a person in such a position to feel free to, e.g. stop doing this or that, for he alone is involved in his reasons for doing it, and there is no question of his being unfree. Though of course a decision could still amount to unkindness. Co-ordination would be impossible, though a semblance of concerted action would obtain if a number of individuals severally and independently aimed at the same thing. But in such cases there is only a semblance of co-operation for the dovetailing of efforts would always be an accident of separate reasons of separate people happening to be similarly directed. A deterministic psychologist could perhaps produce some reliable predictions, but this is another thing altogether. After all even completely unco-operative weather can be predicted in some circumstances.

Genuine co-operation and co-ordination can begin only where one independent individual can count on what the other independent individual will do, and count on him acting towards a certain end for a certain reason. My counting on water quenching my thirst is not a basis of co-operation, nor does one co-operate with a car simply because one can predict its "behaviour." Only if the above stated condition is satisfied is it *unnecessary for each* individual to *bear in mind every aspect of the situation.* Only in this case can individuals specialise, for then one can do what one is supposed to do in the knowledge that the other part of the job will be attended to. Not unless people can count on the performance of others are they free from worrying about its occurrence, and can co-operate by concentrating on their own part of the bargain. According to the formula cited above even if the individuals are in a very good sense independent, some of their actions come to be dependent on others, viz. on their wishes, and the wish-holders are secure in this knowledge.

If I envisage two people where A's determination to e.g. remove a stone, is the reason for B's so acting, the desired situation obtains. If B accepted A's wish as his reason for acting, his reason stands as long as A's wish stands. Thus were A to know what the situation was he could rely on B's co-operation. *This is a good reason* for believing that he will not cease, *regardless of A's wishes.* One could not put absolute reliance on this, B could decide that he is not any more concerned with A's wishes, and walk off. Such might be the tale of any voluntary co-operation.

If the above qualification appears severe and limiting let me observe that to have a good reason for counting on someone's co-operation is vastly different from not having any reason at all; it is this difference that is crucial to our study. For now we have a relation which gives us a basis in which efforts of several individuals can be: co-ordinated, directed towards a common goal, special tasks apportioned, support ensured. As long as individuals remain free, it is impossible to make absolutely certain that they will keep faith; why they do so is not a subject of this study. But it is important that individuals can keep faith; that now we know what basically takes place when they do, and what basically happens when people count on others keeping faith. This deals with a problem that worried Hobbes – Wherein lies our guarantee that others will respect us and our safety? The answer: they accept our wishes in this respect as a reason for doing so. Hobbes would not be satisfied, he wants to know what ensures that they will accept our wishes in this fashion. It should be agreed that *no further assurances can be given* and the risk that is left is just the normal hazard of life, and not a very high one at that. Furthermore, it might very well be that this risk is beneficial, because it is only another aspect of the necessary flexibility of communal life (*vide* defunct laws).

If A's wishes are in a positive way[6] *B's reason for doing this or that, we have a relation that leads to co-operation. If on top of this both A and B know that this is the case, and furthermore if both know that both do, we do have some form of co-operation.*

In the intermediate cases where for example A knows what B's reasons are, but this is unknown to B, the position seems intermediate and would be more misleading than helpful to insist here that it is either the case that there is, or that there is not co-operation between A and B. Either decision is likely to lead to counter-intuitive results in further argument, so let us agree to call it a twilight zone and leave it at that. It might be helpful to settle the question on the occasion of empirical study, but it will be better also to be guided by empirical results in reaching such a decision.

We are of course happier to speak of co-operation where the aim is, so to speak, mutually agreed upon, for we sometimes loath to use the word "co-operation" where the traffic is completely one-sided. This we shall ignore in the interests of simplicity. Three points need stressing here: (a) One has to be capable of rudimentary co-operation be fore one is in a position to envisage, discuss or achieve mutual agreements. (b) The position might be mutual in a simple way whenever B can count on A as much as A on B. This can come about naturally, for example if the stone half blocks A's door and B's door and could clear either by blocking completely the other; A and B could have similar but different wishes which they could accept mutually – in trying to push the stone across the path. (c) The same or identical, wish can inform the actions of several people. Thus co-operation can exist between groups of individuals. This makes it adequate as a basis of communal life, for a community needs to involve more than just a pair of people.

Given that we have co-operation we can distinguish several distinct levels of it. To start with we can have *sporadic co-operation*. This exists where several people co-operate on a *single immediate task* without generalising either their method or relationship. An example is provided by several people forming a chain to pull a child out of a swift current. Here the task and its entirely mutual wishes are immediately present

[6] *Vide* p. 10 where this q ualification is introduced.

to all participants during the whole, relatively short, time of co-operative effort, and it need not mature into a policy of forming a chain again in similar circumstances.

Contrast this with an effort of building a dam, a job that will last several days; it is still a reasonably immediate and single task, but the participants go to other tasks and occupations and return to this one several times, and during that time they are a kind of organised unit composed of several individuals. To introduce a technical term, an *ad hoc structure* exists if this set of inter-individual relations endures for some time but relates to several actions jointly directed towards a given specific end. The structure is *ad hoc* precisely because it comes into being with relation to a particular goal, which is the occasion for the arrangement, and ends when the goal is attained. And it is team structure rather than simply an arrangement, because the arrangement binds the individuals beyond the one temporal occasion of co-operation. When the end is achieved the agreement, and the team, come to an end – the path is clear; the barn is built, the workers disperse, etc. A simple co-operative action, and an *ad hoc* co-operative team agreement, are clearly distinct levels of co-operation, though both are relatively simple and narrow.

An arrangement need not be directed towards a specific job, which has a specified clear end to it, so a third level of co-operation becomes both possible and desirable. As an example let us suppose that a majority of individuals in a group agreed that a widow of any of the group members should be looked after following her husband's death, and that everybody should see to it. If all acted on this wish, then if the need arose, anybody would help a woman for this reason *whenever* she was left widowed by the death of one of the group members.

Here the agreement is not directed *ad hoc* towards a particular contingency and/or goal. Not only different performances are required in different cases but each of them has a separate though similar end, to wit that a widow should be looked after. *A standing arrangement* seems a natural name for this. In a standing arrangement the *kind of action* is related to the *kind of occasion*, viz. whenever you see an officer, salute; whenever you make a promise, keep faith; etc. Thus the arrangement is generalised, for it appertains to occasions *re* their general character, for example, as being a case of promise giving, and it is universalised in that it applies to all such occasions.

So far we have distinguished (a) *a sporadic co-operation* – this has very limited range; (b) *ad hoc team arrangement* – has a wider range, but is still immediately geared to a definitive project; it is a more extended plan, but it is a specific plan with a definitive product envisaged as a reward for the completed job; and (c) *a standing arrangement* – that has a different and much more sophisticated point. Its point is to keep things going in a certain way, for example, to provide security and peace between people. And as long as e.g. chivalry is the rule, ladies need not worry about obtaining seats in trains. At this stage, unlike the other two, it begins to make sense to talk of having policies, general aims, etc.

The capacity for sporadic co-operation is presupposed both in *ad hoc* team arrangements and standing arrangements. In actual development all the stages might well arise simultaneously. but the conceptual point is valid independently. One has to have the capacity to simply take another's wish as one's reason for acting if one is to have the capacity to take someone's standing wish to the effect that whenever O then A.

Where there are standing arrangements a b c . . . n, one can organise one's life counting on the presence of whatever they provide. So an above-mentioned prospective widow, can count on the support of other members of the group, and she can plan with that in mind, and so can a prospective dead husband. For unless standing arrangements are entered into and terminated frivolously they will create a reliable set of conditions within which framework an individual will be able to organise his own life. The creation of such a situation is basically the purpose for which any community is brought into being.

I have made the qualification against frivolity for of course the fact that an arrangement is standing does not automatically ensure its acceptance or continued acceptance. But it would be pointless and frivolous to enter into such an agreement for an instant of time, for then both the generality and universality of the arrangement would be rendered futile. A standing arrangement has to be provided with sufficient scope with regard to its purpose and nature. For example we might have a standing arrangement for the duration of the game, but then its scope is severely limited, this alone will rule it out as a basic communal arrangement.

It should be noted here that no claim is made at this stage that arrangements are sufficiently well described to show the working of a community. A number of points have to be made to achieve this result – this will come later. At the present stage elements, for example standing arrangements, are presented as possible elements or possible necessary elements of communal structure, references to being for example "a communal arrangement" refer to this fact and should be readily understood, but will be defined later more precisely and accurately.

Standing arrangements, unless they are futile or defunct, demand either action or refraining from action at least sometimes. As a consequence of their generality and universality the number of actions demanded is not specified, but we must act every time when appropriate situations arise – one might never meet a General, or meet one every day – one salutes when one meets one. If the occasion envisaged, for example meeting Julius Caesar, could never take place, then the arrangement would be futile in principle. Standing arrangements have regulations as their counterpart – for in these terms people are required to be methodically repetitious, and such *a requirement is a regulation.*

It seems clear that Winch is wrong in holding, in apparent agreement with Weber, that any action with a sense must be the application of a rule, since it must *commit* the actor "to behaving in one way rather than another in the future."[7] The foregoing discussion shows firstly that any such commitment is a result of adopting a certain type of reason for action *viz.* of the wish of another, or of a communal wish and not of an action done on this or another occasion, further it is clearly the case that co-operation is prior to the existence of rules or regulations. It is easy however to see the initial plausibility of the criticised view if one remembers that in stating it no distinction was shown between rules and arrangements. Once this is done it becomes clear that co-operation is the basic and minimal sensible (sinnhaft of Weber's) social or interpersonal act. This fact might be obscured if the illustration is taken from actual sophisticated cases, these e.g. an economic act, will involve more than sporadic co-operation, and would certainly involve rules.

It is not precisely clear what Winch means by "application of a rule." In the weakest sense it could be an action with an eye to the future, but without system or repetitiveness. If so his view is trivially true. If on the other hand, by "rule" we mean something displaying generality of aim and application, then the idea is clearly dubious. There is no reason to believe that deliberately repetitive action is the

[7] *Vide* P. Winch, *The Idea of a Social Science and its Relation to Philosophy*, p. 50 ff.; also M. Weber, "R. Stammler's Ueberwindung der Materialistischen Geschichte-Auffassung" in *Gesammelte Aufsätze zur Wissenschaftslehre*, Mohr, 1922.

conditio sine qua non, or the only form of a structure minded action, in fact the opposite is the plausible view. Besides this, to be able to apply a rule is a matter of relative sophistication, and it is therefore unsatisfactory to select it as the unanalysed basis of social theory, yet it is a strong temptation to which I have succumbed at an earlier stage.[8] The above discussion is an attempt to provide a more satisfactory basis. Here the unanalysed foundation consists in the assumption that a person is capable of two things: (a) of forming a wish with regard to an action and its aim (b) of forming at least sometimes, a satisfactory opinion of another person's wish. These are not matters of social and behavioural sophistication, which is not to say that they cannot be problems for psychology or philosophical psychology – but in social theory it appears reasonable to accept these as basic facts.

Who requires one to follow a regulation? In the cases we were envisaging one just accepts another's wish as one's reason. If this wish is such as to require a standing arrangement – this wish is the reason for one's methodically repetitious performance – the acceptance of that wish does then establish the regulation in question. In this way at least the question: "What is the basis of the regulation?" is settled. For if the wish *is accepted* the relevant individuals will act on it (since it is their reason for acting) and the arrangement is in force.[9] The "mechanism" involved is obvious once it is thought of, for it would simply be inconsistent to accept e.g. B's standing wish that everyone should salute any statue of King Arthur, and then to refrain from saluting on being confronted with such a statue. Saluting on appropriate occasion is then a requirement of consistency and is an obvious consequence of the appropriate acceptance of the standing wish in question. Given this acceptance the question: "Why should I salute this statue now?" is settled. Other questions are not thereby settled, *viz.* Why should people accept the wish? What guarantee do we have that the wish is or will continue to be accepted? etc. The first of these is only marginal from our point of view, the second touches on the problem of reliability. The answer to the second is not easy, but seems needed.

We might suggest, to anticipate some of the points to come, that the fact that such reliance is placed is just a brute fact at the most basic level. Further, where any group structure exists, and a number of individuals are involved, the system of regulations acquires a sta-

[8] Cf. my article, "Basic Political Concepts," *Philosophical Quarterly*, 1963.

[9] There is no objection to saying that to accept the relevant standing wish is to "internalise" the regulation in question.

bility of its own. The fewer the people involved, the fewer the regulations accepted; the more *ad hoc* and less enduring the arrangements, the less reliable they would be. At best individuals would act as stabilising influences on each other. For it is unlikely that all will want to go off in the same direction, and generally it is a fact that the majority of them have a stake in preserving most of the regulations intact.

We need standing arrangements for the existence of a community. But the existence of some standing arrangements is not enough. For Jack could do something because Jill wanted him to do it; Jill could do something because Barbara would be upset if she didn't, etc. However many such mutual respect arrangements there are, and however many of them are standing, if it does not go beyond particular wishes of particular persons or arrangements concerning only very small sets of individuals within the group, it cannot be regarded as involving the people in a set of communal arrangements.

In the absence of general group rules, how could there be a community? For the sake of clarity it would be best to say that in the above mentioned case we have a group of individuals, but a community does not exist. Thus minimally "group" is to be taken as meaning no more than just a collection of individuals remaining in some kind of contact with each other, over a period of time. This does not imply any communal structure, if by such structure we mean a set of regulations aiming at a common end, or setting up the guidelines of communal life. In the above cited case no such guidelines exist, yet the individuals stand in some significant relation to one another.

Could people capable of accepting regulations form a group as primitive as that? It seems logically possible to have one composed of such relatively sophisticated individuals. If the regulations concerned only a very small number of individuals each; if furthermore they concerned only trifles – one would not be tempted to call the resultant group a community. If *all* members could count on general co-operation in some types of contingency, one might be tempted to apply this name, but this is not quite enough either, for it seems important that these accepted "wishes" should not be completely capricious and irrelevant to such central issues as people's safety and means of livelihood. It is possible to think of a type of regulation no number of which would produce a community. For example, take the following code: Anyone can do anything to anybody provided he clasps his hands twice afterwards or three times before. Clearly this arrangement is futile in that one might rely on people's observance of it and yet nothing would be established that would either facilitate one's life, or make it more difficult. If arrangements are to lead to communal structure, at the very least they must make a difference. This is the minimal requirement, but it might well be the case that they must also make a specific kind of difference.

Now suppose that we have a number of standing "wishes," leading to standing arrangements that do make a difference, established in a group of individuals. They are understood to involve most of the members of the group. The rules that express them could be regarded as communal rules, related to communal expectations. For the significant thing about such a state of affairs is that those wishes are accepted by every or by most members of the community as reason for acting in a given way in appropriate circumstances. It would be then both misleading and inaccurate to single out a special individual as the person whose standing wish was being followed. Clearly if such an individual dies the expectations do not die with him. A communal wish is more permanent than an individual one, it is possible to put it in the following way. An individual accepting a communal wish *a* as a reason for acting can be taken to surmise that all, most, or an important (sufficient) proportion of members of his community wish people to x in circumstances, x and this is his reason for acting. This creates a problem, for this account presupposes an already existing community, but it is easy to see that there is no serious difficulty involved. One can easily imagine a process in virtue of which a transition from a loose group of individuals co-operating singly, led to them having communal status and communal expectations because a number of wishes came to be shared between individuals, and since it is then immaterial to specify whose wish one follows, a reaction to group-wishes *per se* comes slowly into being.

We may put our findings fully in the following manner. *We can have a community basically among people who are capable and willing to take the wishes, expectations, beliefs and attitudes of other people as at least part of their reasons for acting in this, that or another manner. It exists if and when among a group of such people there are non-capricious significant communal expectations and when many of such expectations are treated positively as reasons for acting by members of the community, provided that this takes the form of standing arrangements, expressible in rules.*[10]

[10] No useful distinction can be drawn here between the arrangement working and people having duties.

This needs to be qualified. An institution, a body, or an organisation such as e.g. Shell Co. of Australia, or the legal profession of U.K., are not communities in the basic sense, though they might sometimes be usefully likened to one, yet they are groups organised according to the above precept. One wishes to say that they are sub-groups that exist in communities. This distinction is not easy to draw, but it might be useful at this stage to say that a community is usually thought of as comprising a number of arrangements sufficient for its members to base the organisation of their whole lives at least broadly on it. Later a much fuller discussion of this point will be provided.

To come back to our orginal line of thought, it is only when communal expectations lead to standing arrangements that we can talk of communal rules or regulations, and the beginning of community, because below this level stability in time is either impossible or purely accidental, i.e. not reliable.

It is not claimed that such regulations must be explicitly formulated, promulgated, agreed, etc. They exist when in terms of people's behaviour the communal expectations are treated in fact as standing reasons for action by the members of the group. It is not required that every expectation should be *at all times* accepted as a good reason for doing this or that, nor yet that *everybody* should accept every one of them. A community exists if, and *only* if there are both a sufficient number of such communal expectations *and* a sufficient number of the members of this group take a sufficient number of them as reasons for acting a sufficient number of times. Thus the situation may be rather complex, some expectations being better established, more strictly observed, others less well-known, etc. but it must be possible to discern the effect of those observances among the members of this community who must be able to count on the continued performance of actions prescribed in terms of the said arrangements.

It is not claimed that these judgments are always easy to make in practice, yet the ideas of sufficiency in numbers, stability, etc. are frankly practical. An arrangement is sufficient if, and only if, it is possible and reasonable to make a habit of acting in accordance with it. Thus the origins of the Hobbesian point of the necessity of the effectiveness of arrangements are explained. This is well illustrated by the old story about lying – if deception was the rule it would be unreasonable to take it seriously for in the absence of the practice of honesty even attempts at deception are almost completely futile – thus the futility of many modern international dialogues, and of a great deal of advertising.[11]

A community permits orderly life, organised on stable and formalised lines. Obviously a single standing arrangement affects only one narrow aspect of life and will do nothing of the kind. Communal arrangements cannot be narrow or futile, and what is more, they must occupy important enough a position for at least the majority of the broadly significant interpersonal relations in that group to be informed by the arrangements, and for basic personal arrangements to revolve around them.

What I have in mind is as follows: It is possible to have sporadic cooperation with others, and this might be important. It is also possible to be in the habit of cooperating with others. This kind of "alliance" can become very important to the participants. Further, and importantly either of the two types of cooperation can occur in this, that, or another sphere. If we take an individual, what he does in the course of his life can be divided into a finite number of spheres of action and interest. Thus he has a job, a hobby, indulges in recreation, looks after his health, has family responsibilities, etc., etc. Clearly when habitual cooperation is limited to one sphere only, the participants are more independent than united, if it were to comprise all possible spheres – they would form a cohesive unit - between lies a scale affording many possibilities. A good example is provided by relations between states; on one hand we have a pact, e.g. a trade agreement, on the other a complete union; the question is where does a single political unit emerge? Clearly there is no simple arithmetical answer, but we can say broadly that a community exists when the spheres of action covered by standing arrangements between members are either considerably more important, or more numerous or both than those left out. If this answer is found too vague, solace might be found in the fact that if it was much more precise it would almost certainly fail to be true to life and relatively useless in practice – crippling precision is the counterpart of futile vagueness; between the Scylla of one and the Charybdis of the other lies good sense.

In practice it is always significant, and often decisive, whether the individuals themselves regard the existing arrangements as the backbone of their relations with others. What will satisfy a New Guinea savage will not do for a Swedish intellectual. It is important also to note the scope and nature of other inter-personal relations existing be-

[11] Alternatively, this is why advertising sells not by what it says, but by how it says it.

tween the individuals in question. The dominant position of this or that set of arrangements must depend *inter alia* on these two factors and is a matter of judgment that cannot be settled in principle.What is more, empirical factors are here of prime importance so it might not be feasible for a philosopher to attempt to solve such problems, he can hope at best to begin the search and offer guidelines.

Let us then continue towards the analysis of possible communal systems. Every standing arrangement as cited above is likely to have definitive repercussions in conduct, for in terms of such an arrangement one might be required to do something, prevented from doing something or obtaining something etc. Such things naturally regulate our conduct. Expressions stating the respective arrangements, and proscribing such effects, can be called *regulations*. Where there are a number of communal regulations it is possible to distinguish three distinct orders of complexity.

Firstly, the existence of no more than separate regulations i.e. a number of regulations totally unrelated to each other, each of them dealing with a completely different matter and a completely different aspect of life. Regulations that were not from different areas could not be separate in the required sense, for if they concern connected matters there is always the possibility of one influencing the effect of another.

Such a mere collection of regulations is insufficient to support or form a community for the rules would have almost no joint effect, thus failing to unite members of the group in an appropriate manner. To be sure they would make life easier if they were any good, they might increase the safety of individuals and certainly would make some measure of reliance on the actions of others possible. But to make life easier is not necessarily to make it communal. Arrangements that form the backbone of a community must have some unifying effect, at least sufficient to permit common aims and actions. If the arrangements are so far apart as to make interference between them impossible, their effects on the life of the group could be only sporadic, resulting in an almost non-arrangement from the overall point of view.

No group deserves the name of "community" unless it is capable of communal (common) action and communal aims. Even assuming that the existing independent regulations are each accepted by all or most members of the group, this will not make such aims and actions possible. The reason for this will become more apparent after the discussion of codes. Here it will suffice to note that the group would at best display common reactions. Each regulation deals characteristically with a particular type of contingency, e.g. if someone is drowning give him help. If it dealt with more it would be in fact a set of directives not one directive, and strictly and pedantically speaking would involve a set of regulations, most simply a conjunction of them. Now a single directive allows no play whatever, there are only two possibilities either it is obeyed or it is disobeyed – on this a common aim cannot be built. To have a common aim – to engage in common endeavour is to adopt, to pursue a goal, to be able to do this is to be able to select one, to be able to decide on and to implement a policy. With a single regulation to disobey is to break away, to obey is to accept a standing arrangement – there is no room for forming a policy.

It could be argued that the existence of a standing arrangement is a proof of the existence of a policy or at least of a goal. Now in a sense the two are of a kind, in both cases more than one individual aims at something in common. But it is clear that even if there is a similarity there is also a difference when we talk of a community being able to act as a unit, we mean capable of reacting beyond the mere and blind application of a single rule. We require that the policy is orientated in a broader sense, that it covers or at least is capable of covering an area of activity. Communal policy could possibly concern a single contingency in one case or another, but the possibility of communal action cannot be limited to single contingencies.

Secondly, regulations can form a cluster. Regulations in a cluster are seen to be related to each other; they can be consistent, inconsistent with each other, they can support, supplement, or limit each other. These relations must be understood in terms of the effects they have on the behaviour of individuals. Take a regulation stating that one should not get out of bed before 7.00 a.m. and another requiring people to have showers before sunrise. If the sunrise was at 5.00 a.m. then the regulations would be contradictory for, to comply with the second would mean breaking the first. Regulations can also implement each other. We have a case of direct implementation where for instance, the first regulation says that one has to wash in the morning, and the second regulation that after one has complied with the first, one ought to dress.

Regulations can also support each other in a less definitive manner. A regulation might direct politeness to ladies, another might say that it is impolite to discuss medical matters at dinner time. The two have a joint effect, for if I break the second regulation in the presence of ladies, I have broken the first as well. Similarly, for regulations limiting each other. If one regulation states that women should not appear in public nude, and another that in the case of emergency decency regulations do not apply, then in a case of fire a woman is permitted to appear in public in the nude not because decency regulations permit this, but because they are stated not to be applicable. In this case the second regulation is directly framed in order to limit the first. But we can have a limiting influence of a less definite kind. Thus, if of two rules, one forbids the telling of lies, and the second bars doing harm to others, cases may arise in which when I follow the one I am infringing the other. Thus if I refrain from lying to a patient I might scare him and do damage to his health, and conversely if I refrain from harming him in that way I will tell a lie. Here the regulations are not framed with the view to limit each other, but in at least some situations they cannot both be obeyed. Precedence need not be established and then it is left to our discretion and judgment what we will do in each particular case of conflict. This is important in practice for it is impossible to take several rules seriously and to refrain from considering them together and weighting them against each other in cases of conflict; in a cluster this is unavoidable, for there the regulations are more or less independently conceived and framed without precise regard for their effects on other rules. This state of affairs is common in naturally grown as opposed to contrived, sets of rules – customs, and more importantly, morals, being good examples. This leads to dilemmas, but need not be a failing of the system, on the contrary, completely precise determination might be bad. Taking the flexibility of the situation into account, the need and scope for judgment might be all to the good, and even more so if we were to maintain, for example, that moral problems are essentially particular.[12] But, of course, the more of conflict cases, the more need for direct judgment, the nearer our rules come to be guidelines and less, prescriptions. In a really drastic case they might fail to be either.

We can now say that *we have a cluster of regulations if the regulations considered affect each other and have a joint effect on those guided by all of them.* At this stage the regulations are no longer separate, and we are at a more sophisticated level than hitherto. Clusters admit of varying degrees of complexity and sophistication, some of what is not possible with single regulations becomes possible where clusters of them are concerned.

A cluster of regulations can cover a separate area of behaviour and it

[12] Which seems to be a most plausible proposal – if so, "A System of Ethics" is a significant misnomer.

can be known to cover it. If so, a regulation either belongs to the cluster or cannot be accepted as proper. As examples of such areas let us think of behaviour at meals, at the football field, courting etc. Now we are involved in a *third order of complexity*. It is not enough anymore that a regulation would interfere with other regulations already in the cluster in order to be relevant, it must be admitted to membership, by (e.g.) a rule of admittance, and then the cluster becomes like a club that can veto and accept members.

This type of arrangement will typically exist if regulations in the collection are designed to jointly control the area or are accepted as doing so. The design need not be a deliberate one but the authority of the given set of rules over the area must be accepted. Consequently, if one knows all the regulations in the set, in which not one is applicable to the action he is contemplating he will for that reason know that he is at liberty to do as he likes.[13] This is not to mean that the cluster of rules concerning our table cannot be over-ridden by the rules of morality or the rules concerning emergency or similar, but only that normally when and if we regard table manners as important we will think only of what the cluster of rules concerning manners at the table enjoins us to do. I shall call this area-covering cluster *a code*. No regulation in a code is independent, this mutual and essential inter-dependence of its component regulations is the code's other hallmark. If these conditions are satisfied, an entry of a regulation into a code might be formalised further, and in more sophisticated cases generally will be, but this is not essential, even if advisable on practical grounds.

I am well aware that it may not be easy to determine what counts as this or that *separate* area in which certain rules might be operative, and that the existence of a cluster of rules might be one of the important factors which makes us decide that it is in fact a separate area. But by and large it is clear what is meant when we say that this set of rules covers this or that area of behaviour, so there is a good *prima facie* case for the suggested usage.

Obviously we have important areas of behaviour concerning particular needs of the body, thus eating, sex and illness behaviour form natural divisions. There are also well recognised differences between

[13] This is one of the reasons why morality cannot be ultimately rule based, for this does not follow in ethics, though moral rules might form a system, albeit a loose system, a sophisticated cluster, but not really a proper code, unless the fact that it implements a frame of mind is taken as a test of membership and the cluster seen as a system of rules accepted by all right-minded men. The problem lies in the fact that not all right-minded men agree on all moral matters.

things like hunting, things like fishing, things like farming and things like stealing. It is my contention that such discernment is sufficient for the formation of codes of behaviour. For a distinction which makes practice possible is clearly sufficient. We might experience some difficulty in dealing with this problem. Areas can arise slightly differently with slightly different practical ramifications. There are cases in which it might be hard to decide what we want to say no matter what our original definitions were. None of this need amount to a practical difficulty, there need be no *felt* complexity from the point of those who form and obey codes of behaviour. The *existence* of a code need not be affected by this type of difficulty but the grasp of the limits and the nature of a particular code will be.

Approaching the matter in an analytic frame of mind it is possible to discern a large number of divisions into different areas of behaviour. Nonetheless those who live in a society do not usually view this imposing array with dismay, indeed they are mostly unaware of its existence. Codes are developed between individuals that have sympathetic "rapport" with each other – if they didn't they would not begin to cooperate. As the cooperation develops so does a common outlook. Individuals need not react identically but in sympathy with each other, i.e. they tend to think on the same lines even if their ideas differ. Thus it is very likely that what will appear as belonging to one area of behaviour to one, will appear so to others. The process is strengthened by the formation of clusters of regulations and codes – in this differences can be ironed out. A division of activities in different spheres can thus emerge without any consciousness of even the possibility of alternatives, indeed this tends to be the rule.

Coming back to the intellectual difficulty, it can be attacked by saying that with respect to any set of clusters of regulations and/or codes what are different areas of behaviour is determined by what is so regarded by those who live according to the relations in question. This reply will not quite do, for an anthropological study might fail to provide a clear answer. Further if we wish to compare it might be advisable to compare the actuality of various practices with what is possible and possibly with what gives greater clarity. These are difficult problems but they need not be considered now.

For the present purpose it is enough to establish what a code of behaviour is like. We need not always agree on what an area of activity is. But if this or that is regarded as an area then a code of behaviour with respect to it must cover it, and cover it in such a way that the members of the respective groups regard it as having authority in dealing with this area. Thus even if the idea of an area of behaviour were flexible and largely a matter of convention it would be possible to tie the concept of a code to a concept of an area of activity. The idea that a certain activity forms a certain separate area and a code to regulate this type of behaviour may grow together. For instance a growing cluster of regulations as defined before might come to be regarded as increasingly having a definite *gestalt* characterizing the activity which comes under its influence. When this becomes explicit enough in the minds of people concerned, the activities affected by the said cluster may come to be regarded as a separate area of activity, and then the cluster will assume the character of a code provided only that it is regarded as *the set* of regulations that control this area.

Is the existence of a significant code sufficient to form a communal bond between people? In a limiting case, all communal activity could be regarded as one area, and then all communal regulations would have to be regarded as a single code. I am not arguing that communities of that sort exist, nor am I expressing any doubts as to whether they exist. But if we were to discern a group of people who had a cluster of regulations controlling all their communal activities and regarded communal activities as a separate and single area, then the whole bond between the members of this community would be this single code, provided only that the code affects sufficiently the conduct of members to become a decisive factor in the planning of their respective lives. When the effect of a set of regulations in an area of behaviour is significant in the required sense, it is a matter of judgment, and is bound up in practical considerations and actual conditions as per each case.

An example might clarify the point. Envisage a code consisting entirely of the following regulations:

(a) Serve the ladies first,

(b) Eat always with a covered head,

(c) Don't put your feet into the food,

(and that includes all tacit agreements as well).

The statement: "Their code of manners consists in a, b, and c" is intelligible, but there is no quarreling with the statement that they have no manners either. Just think of what they are permitted to do, e.g. put the remains of their food into their neighbour's plates; force them down their throats, etc. Their code is not significant, certainly not by any standards that we are prepared to regard as reasonable.

A code is significant when it is at least worth the trouble of taking it up. This is true about a regulation as well, but here it is a much more important point since the code is understood to have sovereignty over its area and *omission amounts to permission*. It might be as well to remember that what might look insignificant to us, need not look so to others.

A system in which vendetta and taboo are the only law and the only moral code, might well seem completely useless till we experience the absence of any system. This is one of the reasons why the actual and practical character of the judgment involved is insisted upon.

In a system of regulations sufficient to form a community, it is possible to discern at least one more factor. The range of activities will differ from culture to culture and to some extent from person to person, but there is a number of types of action which most if not all members of any group have to perform from time to time in order to live, and to live reasonably well. These usually include upbringing of children, family relations, provision of food, security and shelter, etc. It will be obvious that any arrangements that will leave the majority of such problems untouched will affect the lives of those involved only marginally.

It should also be noted that certain areas must be covered lest anarchy in this area will lead to general anarchy. Security within the group is obviously a case in point and there might be others.[14]

It is basic to the concept of "community" that the regulations and agreements existing between individuals in a group will justify it being called the name if they can be regarded as: forming general guidelines; providing the limits; and generally creating a structure in response to which the lives of its members are moulded. Again what might seem complete anarchy to some might appear a secure heaven to others, so there is a range of possibilities. However, the point allows of objective interpretation and is not the sole province of a philosopher for such problems involve empirical matters, an area where others are expert. A community will be formed only if we have a significant number of regulations ranging over a significant number of suitable areas.[15] Again it has to be remembered that what is significant will be to some extent at least determined by what the participants are prepared to regard as such.

One test of whether or not this is the case might consist in asking

[14] But Hobbes was surely wrong if he thought that controlling this area alone is sufficient to form a community.

[15] I put it this way to allow for a community where we have no codes, only a cluster of regulations.

whether a member of such a group will have to re-orientate his style of living, i.e. re-shape and re-formulate his ways of dealing with every-day contingencies if he were to abandon communal life, or accept membership of another and different group. The question is not as to whether any changes are necessary, but as to whether a drastic change is. On the whole unless abandonment of the group's arrangements leads to such basic adjustment, the group is not a community. What would be drastic enough for the purpose is again a matter of judgment but this is neither fatal nor surprising.

Communal structure depends at the very least on codes of behaviour, but in most cases it is seen to involve also some further and more sophisticated elements. Importantly a code, i.e. a cluster of regulations covering an area of activity, has an effect as such consisting in the joint effect of all the component regulations. It works as a single unit, and is regarded as having an aim of its own. These are two aspects of one and the same feature; namely that a code is a purposeful structure, not merely a collection or a group of purposeful regulations; i.e. a deliberate structure. It need not be deliberately designed as such but is manifested in the fact that the relations between member regulations serve a purpose in the same sense in which each particular regulation serves a purpose. In a mere cluster other regulations are to be regarded as conditions in which the given regulation operates, but in a code these relations are as much a part of the system of behaviour control as the regulations themselves.

We can talk about the purpose of a code, and of a regulation, but not of a cluster of regulations. A regulation has a particular purpose, *viz.* to stop people from going unwashed to bed – it controls a particular type of contingency in a particular way. A code *implements a policy* – it consists of a number of regulations that jointly have a general effect on the behaviour of the controlled individuals in a given area of activity, for example, in football it can be intended to promote team-work, to penalise unskilled handling of the ball and to prevent the match from deteriorating into a series of wrestling matches. The same area can of course be controlled for different reasons and with different aims. Importantly a single regulation could not have as its purpose that, for example, a football match should be a team rather than an individual effort.[16] A particular regulation however can enhance this tendency of the code. If a regulation belongs to a code this tendency to enhance this or that effect of the code is as important a reason for its acceptance

[16] This will be qualified later in the discussion of maxims.

as its direct aim. Since we regard them as forming one code we regard each of the regulations against a background of the overall effect, and this is the new attitude. For instance, we could say about a regulation permitting on-the-spot fines that it is inconsistent with the code to which it is supposed to belong because the general purpose of this code is to safeguard people's liberties and interests as much as it is to regulate their behaviour. Besides establishing a particular effect a member regulation of a code should be directed at furthering the general purposes of the code, and it can do it by determining in a particular way, a particular type of action which may fail under the province of this code. Codes are not merely collections of inter-related rules, but systems of rules, each with a structure, aim and character of its own.

Codes might supplement, contradict or limit each other. For instance we can have regulations concerning manners, and a different code concerning morals. The moral regulations might limit the code of manners in at least two ways: if morals enter the moral code might take precedence over the code of manners, if and when the two overlap. Alternatively regulations concerning manners might not be permitted to deal with moral matters at all. A regulation in terms of manners which says that it is ill-mannered to refuse an immoral invitation from a lady might be inappropriate on this sort of ground. To complicate matters it may be very difficult to know whether a regulation is a moral regulation; whether the problem concerns morals or manners. Nor is it easy to foresee whether what *is* a rule of manners will lead into conflict with morals. Nor again is it the case that a rule becomes a moral rule if it does. But still if an action, activity, case, regulation, clearly belongs to the one area, it will fall under the appropriate code if there is such a code. If actions fall under different codes, then they must be seen as belonging to different areas. And if it is impossible to decide to which area something belongs, it cannot be clear which code should deal with it. Such difficulties do not affect the relations between such terms, they merely make it harder to decide what is the case.

It will be clear that inter-relating codes can support or oppose each other. For, say the legal code can support and in turn be supported by the code of morals; the contrary can also be the case. For instance, it may be illegal to bring certain articles into the country without paying customs duty, it might be nevertheless completely acceptable, in terms of social customs, to lie to the customs officers. But people with delicate consciences might regard this as immoral. In this case morality supports legality and the code of social custom is contrary to both. This is significant for the very same action may be dealt with by these different codes. This need not mean that the codes are not separate, but that they are connected with each other.

As the above example shows that the same action can fall under different codes in a different way, it is therefore difficult to distinguish by reference to areas of behaviour alone. If we say that the area differs according to the question asked *vis-à-vis* the action concerned, we might be accused of begging the question, for what we ask will be naturally determined by the code which we tend to apply in the case under consideration.

Clearly the majority of clear-cut, defining cases falling under a given code belong to a definite area of behaviour – thus obeying orders to: stand at attention; guard the barracks; salute superior officers, etc. are all elements of military behaviour *par excellence*. It is by reference to such typical cases that a code is defined. Once defined it becomes clear that the area has a certain range, and we can judge what falls under it belongs to it. However the range extends beyond clear-cut paradigm cases. When the cases are marginal or in one way or another problematic, conflicts of assessment and area membership can arise. It is also clear that in many of such cases different assessments can be made equally legitimately; this is illustrated by the customs example above. While a complexity is thus introduced we need not be surprised, after all similar problems arise in many different areas, e.g. where relations of general concepts are concerned.

If two codes overlap, i.e. both are relevant with respect to the same action, the point of control must differ from one code to the other. Examples are easy to find. If our morals say that a woman should not undress in front of a man she meets for the first time, this code aims at limiting intimacy to what are regarded as appropriate occasions. Yet a sick-room code (if there is one) would make a refusal by a female patient to undress before a male doctor unreasonable. But the point of stripping here is quite different – it is aimed at facilitating medical examination. Thus more precisely a code consists in *a set of rules aimed at controlling a certain area of behaviour.*

Thus e.g. an action comes under a code of decency or morals when what is done should be treated from the point of view represented by such a code. This point is imperfectly understood by Puritanical people. Even when an action comes under a code the ruling of such a code can be over-ridden: this point is imperfectly understood by many a censor of literature.

With all this we have not eliminated vagueness. There will be difficulties in determining precisely to what type this or that case belongs – is it in bad taste, or simply immoral, to wear a topless dress? Since a case might come under different headings it might be difficult to see what heading should be accepted in this or that contingency. A non-Catholic patient attending a catholic doctor might claim that she wants advice about contraceptives from a medical point of view, and be refused on the ground that the matter is essentially one of morals. It is not my intention to try to resolve all such difficulties, to do so would be artificial and a misrepresentation of an area where fluidity of assessment is both characteristic and important, nor is it always detrimental, for it provides a much needed breathing space.

It must be observed that in any but a marginal case communal structure will involve more than one code. It is also clear that most of such codes will not be independent of each other, they can thus be integrated. When integrated they will form what we can call *a system of codes* or *a system*. When not integrated they will form a *cluster* of codes. The distinction here is drawn on lines similar to the distinction between a cluster of rules and a code – system being a counterpart of the latter. Obviously if two or more codes are integrated and *form a system*, they should only support and/or limit, but should not contradict each other. In practice this perfection need not be reached before we are entitled to say that there is a system.

This point accentuates one aspect of the difference between a code and a mere cluster of regulations, for clusters cannot be related to each other. Related clusters *would have to have a joint affect but can have no territorial rights*, consequently they would form but a single cluster. However they might have areas of concentration. Some regulations belonging to the cluster might be more closely related to each other than to the rest, and there could be more than one such concentrated groups in the cluster. This could be a rise of a gestalt which resembles in form a cluster of codes, it might also be difficult to say which is the case, when the development has progressed reasonably far.

As remarked above there is a similarity between a code and a system; codes not only have a purpose *qua* codes, but are instituted with a view towards furthering the aim of the system as such. Thus one system will be differentiated from another by its purpose and its area of competence, for codes in a system will be area-related as well. Clusters of codes cannot be similary distinguished and if related would tend to form one cluster, composing all the codes in question.

The area covered by a system can be regarded as one main area, divided into sub-areas covered by the codes forming the system. A legal system is a case in point whose sub-areas include: Criminal Law; the Law of Torts; Constitutional Law; Conveyancing, etc. Clearly this process can go on, for there is no reason to believe that only two levels of organisation and of organised areas of activity can be discerned. Thus a social system, or a system of government, can include: legal, economic, defence and other various systems. The complexity and nature of this break-up will of course depend on the facts of the case, and may be different with every social and political structure. Quite obviously, the difficulties in discerning differences between areas and their respective sub-areas can be raised here on a new level of difficulty and complexity. But in principle they are the same as in the cases of different codes, and it would be futile to try to give a more detailed account of them in this place.

Two codes could be completely unrelated to each other. The code of stamp collectors may have nothing whatever to do with the code of courtship, yet both of them be significant for one and the same person, for there is nothing to prevent one from being a collector and courting at the same time, and if he does, he can have time problems. This point is in fact quite important, for it limits the possibility of independence of codes – to see this it is only necessary to think of someone trying to follow at the same time the prescriptions of a serious piano teacher and a serious swimming coach.

The question might arise as to whether in an extreme case a community could not be based on a set of unrelated codes, separately and severally providing the guidelines in respect of which members would base their way of life. In view of all the possible relations and overlaps between codes, this seems extremely unlikely. Even in favourable cases, if what was said above is true, the mere fact that one is spending the minimum reasonable time on one independent activity might interfere with time-requirements of another independent type of pursuit. Thus it is likely that, given that we have number of codes or regulations sufficient to provide the guidelines envisaged as adequate to form the basis of a communal structure, these will be significantly related to each other.

Nonetheless some actions, regulations, codes and, even systems might be independent of the communal structures. To anticipate a future point, if the structure is the ultimate system of codes (systems) and if this system has scope, aim and structure in terms of which arrangements are admitted to the membership of the system, then an existing rule could be outside this system, not affected by its policies and determinations. The rules for brides will provide a ready example from everyday life. Even so the independence is limited, for generally the rule, or rules, will operate in an area left free but not necessarily one where the interference by the community is incompetent.[17] Commonly some general principles or maxims operate in such cases. Riot acts, etc., leave boxing alone, but unless boxing keeps within limits it might fall foul of e.g. the rules concerning manslaughter. Activities and rules might be left outside the communal set-up for many reasons; as a matter of policy, moral, practical, etc., as a matter of custom, or for no reason at all.

Lastly, it might be impossible for public rules to deal with the matter. Private morality comes into the last category, for there is a difference between making someone conform, and making him morally better. If the second is impossible then if what one does affects no one else, and has bearing only on one's own moral standing, no amount of coercion will do any good – this sort of purpose is beyond the reach of communal action. He who does not steal simply and solely to spare his mother worry might be a loving son, but he is still a thief at heart.

The short version of the up-to-date account of "community" can now be given as follows: *A communal structure is the ultimate system of rules, regulations, etc. operative among a group of individuals such that it is this system that provides the bond between them, and is the central unifying factor in their inter-relations, their styles of life and their methods of dealing with at least a large proportion of the most important problems and necessities of life; a community consists of a number of individuals bound together in the above specified way, the communal structure being understood to be the defining feature of their union.*[18]

This "definition" makes it difficult to see how a man could belong

[17] This distinction anticipates a future point *vide* Chapter II under rights against the rules.

[18] Cf. here E. Durkheim, *Elementary Forms of Religious Life*, transl. J. W. Swan, Allen & Unwin, 1915. Durkheim is obviously concerned to relate wishes (beliefs) to communal structure, and to the individual's style of life; he says (p. 10–11) that the individual's way of thinking is dependent upon "the mental state of the group, they should depend upon the way in which this is founded and organised." He takes Religion and Morality to be elements of the "Morphology" of a communal group. These sentiments are akin to some extent to the one expressed here, however due to their generality and relative lack of precision they cannot be accepted as they stand. For instance it is a misconception to equate the set of standing arrangements and rules formative of a community with any separate organised system of beliefs, although in a primitive situation morality and/or religion could be no more than the expression of communal expectation of the kind analysed above. Compare here also: P. Devlin, *The Enforcement of Morals*, O.U.P., 1959, and H. L. A. Hart, *Law, Liberty and Morality*, O.U.P., 1963. These matters will receive further attention in Chapters V and VI.

to several communities, as we seem to be able to say he can. In fact this can be allowed for, at least to some extent, as will become clear in subsequent discussion. However, the specialised usage here advocated tends in fact to be both stricter and narrower than in common parlance. This is accepted for it seems particularly important to demarcate as precisely as possible the community as presented here, since it is the basic socio-political unit. Given this, other uses of the word can easily be regarded as natural *secondary* applications. In this there is nothing either alarming or surprising, for it is a common phenomenon.

The formula presented above is neither perfect nor complete, and the subsequent discussion will seek to supplement and modify it; nor will the end result pretend to anything like completeness, but it is hoped that it might provide a useful starting point, and demonstrate the usefulness of a method.

CHAPTER II

RULES AND RELATED CONCEPTS

It is now necessary to have a more thorough look at some of the concepts that emerged in the previous chapter.

The communal structure is understood and the differences and similarities in kind between communities will most likely be manifested in differences and similarities of rules, codes and systems. Even if the mention of these is insufficient to discuss and exhaust all the social and political problems, they would seem to be involved in a large part of them, and to be essential. For it is hard to imagine a satisfactory theory in the area completely devoid of any reference to these matters.

It might be important to have another look at rules before going on to their combinations and systems.

If a number of standing arrangements are operative in a group of people, the important question is: what sort of bond – what kind of structure do they impose on the members of the community? There are, however, two preliminary questions: (A) *What makes a regulation operative*? and (B) *What sort of effect can a rule have*?

(A.) It can be plausibly stipulated that a regulation is operative if there is *in fact* a standing expectation, e.g. one is expected to avoid hurting others, and if this expectation is *in fact adopted* by individuals as a positive reason for refraining from hurting others. If only two people were involved, the only reason for having confidence in A's and B's observance of the rule could be found in the fact that they have both accepted it. If a number of individuals are concerned multiple relations allowing greater latitude would arise.

As Hobbes saw, the point of having standing agreements is *inter alia*, and importantly, to make resorting to force unnecessary. If it was necessary to appeal directly to force to ensure every single observance of an arrangement – the arrangement would be in effect almost nil. For in such circumstances if the force was insufficient, there would be no performance at all, and if the force was sufficient the arrangement would be largely redundant for the performance could be enforced anyway. However it would be incorrect to hold, as I have held until recently, that this situation would render an arrangement completely futile. An arrangement can be imposed by direct force, this happens if the standing wish is accepted through fear of force being used whenever it is disregarded. While this does not avoid the appeal to force on every occasion it might avoid the actual use of it on most occasions. In the absence of an enforced rule this "economy" could not be effected, but the arrangement is precarious, for the standing wish will be naturally disregarded in almost every case where this could be done safely.[1] To illustrate: suppose that a cave-woman knows that she can expect rough handling if she does not cover the caveman with skins whenever he lies down. If she acts to avoid the threat, we have an *ad hoc* arrangement based on the constant threat of force but not necessarily any actual use of it. If this is all that there is to it, should she realize that the man has grown weaker than she, he would not get any more service. It is instructive to note that the woman's reasons for accepting the arrangement are not germane to its efficiency, only her acceptance of the expectation counts for this purpose. The results are quite sufficient – the cave-man does not need to use force, and he does not need to cover himself. She does what is expected of her because it is expected of her and in the limiting case whenever it is expected of her.[2]

This last point can be generalised – it is always the case that the actual positive acceptance of expectations, e.g. standing communal expectations, is the formally operative factor in a social situation. If in the above case the reason, i.e. fear of direct use of force, renders the arrangement precarious, this is the peculiarity of this case predicated on the very immediate link between the imminent possibility of the use of the force and the positive acceptance of the expectation by the woman. This too can be generalised albeit cautiously. The nature of the reasons leading individuals to accept certain rules will reflect on

[1] Importantly and *inter alia* for this reason enforced arrangements are insufficient to form the basis of a community – there must be internalised arrangements before sufficient "force" can be generated to be significant *vis-à-vis* a communal group of any size. This point will be discussed at a greater length later.

[2] In practice a primitive case of this type might be hard to distinguish from a case of conditioned response, but it is sufficient that the difference between the two cases can be stated clearly, as it can since in the conditioning case reasons need not be mentioned at all, a sufficient explanation being available in terms of causation. In very primitive cases the question of reasons does not even arise, in others it does and we might have to decide whether reasons were operative before deciding how to classify the case. It might well be a matter of some difficulty.

the stability and/or standing of these rules – thus a fanatical attachment might provide an embarrassingly strong bond. Once this point has been noted it becomes obvious that it is not the proper province of a purely theoretical inquiry.

Even though threat of force might be a reason for accepting a rule, clearly it need not be. E.g. where there is already an arrangement between others this may make one drift naturally into accepting it as well. Generally it is to be expected that some point of convenience or prudence is behind the acceptance of rules, particularly since it is difficult to see how compliance with, to say the least, the basic arrangements could be based *on force or threat of force alone* among reasonably large groups of people.

Some important distinctions can be drawn between rules without entering into the field of empirical enquiry. To start with I will designate as *basic* those rules whose existence enables the community to act as a unit sufficiently well to be able to *inter alia* ensure conformity with other rules, that can now be termed *secondary*.[3] It is only now that a distinction can be drawn between those rules that are accepted voluntarily and whose observance depends on the continuation of the good will, and those that depend on other guarantees. *A rule voluntarily observed* is to be normally understood to be a rule that is not a basic rule of the community and is not a rule enforced by the community, but yet is one that is observed by its members.

Why exclude basic rules? If an individual regards himself as a member of a community, this amounts to accepting a set of expectations or wishes as positive reasons for acting. Such a person is community-wish-orientated in the same way that a person could be X's-wish-orientated in another case. In terms of the arrangement to which he is a party, he is no longer free to reject some and to accept some other arrangements from a given set, thus he is *a fortiori* committed to the acceptance of all the basic or essential rules forming this community – he has no freedom left in this respect, or it might be said that entering

[3] It will be clear that this distinction is different from the one drawn by H. L. A. Hart between primary and secondary rules. Cf. here *The Concept of Law*, p. 78–9: "Under rules of the one type, which may well be considered the basic primary type, human beings are required to do or to abstain from certain actions, whether they wish to or not. Rules of the other type are in a sense parasitic upon, or secondary to, the first; for they provide that human beings may, by doing or saying certain things, introduce new rules of the primary type ...."

Clearly the present distinction is not in competition to the one envisaged by Hart.

Problems more akin to those with which he is concerned will be discussed in Chapter VIII below.

the community he has committed himself and has given up his freedom in these matters.

Accepting a code might be a useful illustration of the type of involvement envisaged. Codes have purposes and rules might be either consistent or inconsistent with them. Now if one is aware of the point of the code, for example, to promote team-work on a football field, he will see that actions promoting animosity and distrust between players will be opposed to it. Thus one could be guided even with respect to actions that are not dealt with explicitly in the rules.

While a community does not have a simple purpose like a code, it has its aims and the structure it has represents or implements a policy or policies. More will be said about this later, but it should be noted here that such a policy could be limited to the provision of a *modus vivendi* whereby the several different desires of individuals can be peacefully pursued alongside one another.[4] In fact, no set of rules will be capable of sustaining a community unless such a *modus vivendi* is provided, which is not to deny that it would be possible to suppress a great many desires and aims and still achieve it. To accept membership of the community must involve the acceptance of this general machinery. And this implies, *in consistency*, the *prima facie* acceptance of the basic rules for at least two reasons:– (a) it is not only desirable but necessary to have rules establishing the basic *modus vivendi* and unity, and (b) it is necessary to have community rules (especially of this type) observed. This constitutes a desideratum in matters of this kind even where compliance is not enforced by explicit specific agreements, and sometimes even though it might not be possible to make such explicit provisions. The importance of this point is accentuated when we reflect to what extent what can be termed "a civic spirit" might contribute to communal stability.

One is thus not free *qua* a member of the community to abandon rules dealing with basic matters, and these are for that very reason the community's formation rules. But one can only be said to observe a rule voluntarily if one is free to abandon it on his own cognisance.

This argument leaves a difficulty: it is easy to see how membership of a community will oblige one to support its dictates in general, but the transition from that to the observance of given particular rules and particular codes is less clear. Clearly it would be saying too much to claim that this or that particular rule or set of rules must be accepted

[4] Cf. here the conventionalist view as represented e.g. in A. B. Gibson: "Nature and Convention in a Democratic State," *Australasian Journal of Philosophy*, 1951.

rigidly by all members of the group for such a general reason. In practice unswerving observance is seldom achieved, yet communities thrive.

At least some of the replies that are possible are unlikely to provide realistic machinery guaranteeing in a foolproof way reliable performance, nor can they consist in citing rules formally binding on performers. We are striving to present social relations in general terms, but we can do so without distortion only when we remember that precise statements presuppose particular modes of methodical behaviour on the part of the individuals, and they must be more strict than allowed for by realistic expectation of practical possibility of actual performance. The test of sufficiency of a basic set of arrangements must lie in its actual efficiency. Many various compromises between strict observance of some rules, and some freedom of interpretation are possible and could not be tabulated in advance. It is certain that rigid observance of an extensive set of basic arrangements is sufficient and that this can form an ideal limit. What are the minimal practical conditions is largely an empirical matter, depending on many factors that are best investigated *vis-à-vis* each particular type of situation. A purely theoretical inquiry must be content to state the fairly obvious general conditions. Thus in general terms we can say no more than that a member of a community in virtue of his "acceptance" of its membership is bound to accept a large proportion of its rules but not all of them. If he disregards too many we might say that he is antisocial, at best a communal problem, at worst an enemy of the community. But it has to be remembered that the breaking of a rule is not always the same as abandoning it. Some of the communal arrangements must be basic, others can form a superstructure.

The above cited obligation to comply with rules is of course much stronger and stricter with respect to the basic ones that form the *modus vivendi*, and provide the basic communal cohesion. It is not unreasonable to expect quite strict adherence to these from each member of the community *qua* a member. They are after all the ramifications of active membership. In practice the majority of basic communal rules tend to be so trivial and so ordinary that people do not even notice their existence. For example, we are not conscious of being bound by rules when we refrain from spitting in people's faces, strangling their children, etc. In fact, it requires a considerable effort of imagination in order to envisage a complete absence of all restraint.[5]

Is one bound by a rule only if he accepts the respective communal ex-

[5] Later on a more extended discussion of the grass-roots arrangements will be provided.

pectation as a positive reason for acting in a certain way? In a community of any sophistication there will be a large and complex body of regulations regarded as essential. *All* the people in the community will be expected to conform to at least this set of expectations. Now, insofar as someone is a member of a community, he accepts this general view, and he must regard himself as bound by all regulations of this type even if he does not necessarily regard himself as bound by all regulations current in the community. Now if a member of this community is ignorant of a rule of this type he can be described fairly as being bound by that rule even though he is ignorant and *a fortiori* cannot be said to accept it. This second order commitment presupposes a community which has more than one rule of this type. This then is a less direct and more sophisticated manner in which a regulation can be binding. While substantially correct the above statement is over-simplified and needs qualification. It could be justly objected that a disagreement as to the list of the very basic rules need not render an individual unfit to be a member of a given community. Nevertheless he must agree (a) that there is a set of arrangements on which the community rests, and (b) that it is the existence of a communal belief that a, b, c . . . n, are members of this set that must be regarded as a sufficient reason for acting as if they were. This is so for if the basic set of rules was not thus personinvariant, there would be no basic rules deserving of this name. Members of the community must be able to rely on a, b, c . . . n being accepted as basic, for it is this fact that makes them dependable enough to form the hard core of all the standing cooperative agreements. To say that one should abide by the law of the country is to give articulate thought somewhat loose expression to this basic fact. However since many of the rules of this order are so to say located below the threshold of social consciousness this statement is too limiting. It should be noted here that in practice these demands are likely to be less sharply defined. All factual arrangements tend to be tempered by a consciousness of the limits of profitability and comfort, while at the same time some clearly inessential rules can find their ways into the most privileged company. When people realize that this is the case the status of such a rule is *ipso facto* undermined. In this way change would tend to take place more or less constantly. The analysis attempted here cannot attain transparency unless it treats the structure at least to some extent as if it was static, and to that extent it must oversimplify. The force of the unperceived obligation, our present concern, is based on the criterion of consistency, for it is inconsistent to accept a system S such that F is its *conditio sine qua non* and to reject F at the same time. Practice is the main desideratum here. People's avowals as to what they accept as essential are so often wrong that they must be taken with a grain of salt.

In these terms even though rules can be binding on the ignorant and the unwilling, a rule can be regarded as operative in the *basic* sense if, and only if, the standing expectation which is its basis is on the whole accepted as a positive reason and acted upon by those whom we regard as bound by it. This is independent of any assessment we may have of the causes or reasons of this rule or of any rules being operative.

B. *What kind of effect can a rule have?* Three different types of effect which rules may have on those whose behaviour they aim to control may be discovered: (a) *it can enjoin someone to do something;* (b) it can *leave one free to do something;* and (c) it can *guarantee somebody's enjoyment of something.*

Here again the concept of "force" is based on the criterion of consistency alone, this is the only sense in which I speak of "effect" of rules here and elsewhere.

(a) A rule enjoins someone to do something if in terms of this rule, a performance is expected of him. Thus if A expects B to adopt a certain posture when A says sharply "attention," and if A's expectation is accepted by B as a reason for acting, then this rule enjoins B to this specific performance. Similarly performances are required by standing rules, for example, letting ladies through a door first, and many other actions required upon any occurrence of the appropriate occasions by the rules of chivalry. If such performance is required, we would normally say that that rule imposes a certain *duty* on those bound by it.

A duty *in this sense* is an effect that a rule or a set of rules produces if in consistency it enjoins a person or persons who accept it to do something, e.g. to report for duty daily at 7 a.m. This is basically the case even though, as has been argued above, in some cases a rule might appertain to someone who in a very good sense does not accept it. An example of this is provided by a conscientious objector and his military duty. In these cases the obligation is always second order, though it need not be necessarily weaker. Some further attention will be devoted to such complex cases towards the end of this chapter.

Not every performance that might be required is as specific as indicated above. Consider the rule that in all cases one ought to prefer members of one's own family to others. This may lead to very different cases. Here, to talk about required specific performances would be out of place, it will be impossible to specify in advance what might be required, for there will be an indefinite number of contingencies that might be relevant in various ways to the observance of this sort of rule. This could be usefully termed a general rule, or a *maxim* in contradistinction to a particular rule, or a *regulation*, which controls our behaviour at a particular type of contingency and requires a specific performance. A maxim imposes a general as opposed to a particular duty.

A general duty can be said to constitute a policy – in relevant circumstances act with this in mind, for example, "*salus reipublicae suprema lex esto*." A maxim does not have a policy like a code – it imposes one. Think of possible policies of a football code: that it should put a premium on teamwork, that it should promote skilful handling of the ball, etc. Now to say: "Do everything possible to promote team work" is to impose a goal leaving to the performer the way in which he is going to achieve it; this is a typical feature of maxims and general duties. In contrast, a code will be composed of a number of rules which specify required actions, the outcome of which will achieve something not stated in these rules. A code implements a policy, adding that though codes implement policies, they do not explicitly enjoin us to follow them beyond the instances where particular regulations are operative, we have a reasonably accurate way of talking. We could also express it by saying that the relevant maxim or maxims are or can be meta-rules with respect to a given code (or system).

Particular or general, one possible effect of a rule is to *impose a duty*, thus in relevant cases it would be inconsistent to accept a rule and to fail to do (or refrain from doing) this or that. One cannot claim the freedom to address the Queen by "Hullo Bess sweetie" at the same time as one claims to have accepted the courtier's code of manners.

This consistency point constitutes the rule's imposition of a duty. Those who protest that the point is insufficient to ensure the rule's observance fail to distinguish between what is imposed by a rule as such and the imposition or acceptance by the people of the rule or agreement. Thus while agreeing that the rule: "Do not thwart the natural functions of the body," interpreted as it is by the Roman Catholics, imposes the duty of shunning contraceptives, I am free to use them – I do not have to accept the rule. But I cannot *accept* their rule and feel free to use them at the same time.

It might as well be noted here that the problem of interpretation has to be faced. It is important and difficult where explicit rules are concerned, particularly in cases where a rule is explicitly devised and promulgated, as e.g. in Law. The difficulty thus created makes it necessary to have some other method whereby possible interpretation disputes can be settled. Hobbes of course saw this point and made it the basic concern of his political philosphy.[6] In terms of social engineering it is one of the factors that makes authority and with it status differences necessary, and will be discussed later in this book, particularly, in Chapter Three.

Where non-explicit grass-roots rules are concerned the problem need not be visible at all from the point of view of the members of the community. The arrangements are internalised, or at least can be internalised, in terms of concrete expectations *re* concrete performances, and the verbalised statement of a rule is here naturally secondary – it does not establish the practice, it simply describes it, and if it is unclear we might have a misleading account of it but the rule is unlikely to be misapplied for this reason, unless the misarticulation of the arrangement interferes with our understanding of it, something quite likely to happen in some cases. In any case, a problem may arise for an outsider – e.g. an anthropologist or a sociologist trying to investigate the situation, for he can only grasp the arrangement as far as he can represent it in a rule. This is a difficulty which might make Winch's view[7] seem plausible. Properly understood it offers no solid ground for the belief that only believers and practitioners can understand such things – if it did it would follow that no one properly understands, e.g., promulgated rules and laws at the time when they are promulgated.

(b) A rule might *leave one the freedom* to do this or that. I might be left the freedom to give or to withhold information on certain matters as I please, or to choose any type of transport I like, etc. This happens if there is nothing in the rules that affect me to prevent me from doing this, or from refraining to do it.[8]

Nota bene, it seems impossible to have a rule stating only that no restraint is imposed, for it would be no different from absence of a rule. A rule leaves freedom by being silent, it imposes no restriction beyond what it requires. If the Roman Catholic rule is to go to confession at least once a year, a Catholic is free to go or not to go more often. This freedom might be restricted by another rule. If rules are not deliber-

[6] *Vide* T. Hobbes, *Leviathan*, on Sovereignty.

[7] *Op. cit.*

[8] For this discussion the only relevant limitations of freedom are in terms of rules, the others are another matter altogether.

ately related to each other it is hard to see how this could be prevented, thus a code is required before there can be *a design* to leave one one's freedom.

When there is a code it might be the case that there are no regulations concerning, for example, spending one's holidays, or it might even be the policy implemented by this code to have no regulations concerning such matters, even though they are within its province.

This might be the code-maker's maxim but acceptance of such a maxim is not a necessary condition of his ability to leave such a freedom in fact. If a freedom is only factually there, and is not required by a policy, we should say that the people were given such and such a freedom but not that in terms of this code they had an entitlement to it. For instance where neither the slaves nor their owners recognize any freedom-giving obligations on the part of the owner, slaves can still be granted freedom but only *ex gratia*. If this point seems contradicted by the often cited natural and unrecognised rights and duties, these will be discussed at the end of this chapter, where a contrary stand is taken.

When people are being left freedoms, there is absence of control, but not an entitlement to such an absence. If such entitlement existed, a situation would arise where rules guarantee freedoms, and this is another concept altogether.[9]

A freedom exists when the scope of performances in a given area is determined at least to some extent, and if restrictions do not extend to this, that or another contingency, that could be restricted. The concept of having freedoms makes sense only in contradistinction to being obliged to do something or other, and only if the control that is in fact exercised can be compared relevantly with this particular instance of the lack of control. A freedom is so to say an empty slot in the sense in which linguists use this expression. It would be ridiculous to say that the rule: "Go to the confession at least once a year" leaves one free to watch television after dinner. A rule can be regarded as leaving us our freedom only insofar as it could conceivably restrict it, or insofar as it could support or coexist in one code with a rule that would restrict it. A genuine case is provided e.g. by an Army regulation specifying that soldiers must shower and brush their teeth at 6 a.m. each day, which in absence of further rules leaves them the freedom to

[9] Thanks are due to Professor G. P. Henderson, the editor of *Philosophical Quarterly*, for the permission to reprint the next section, which appeared under the title *Rights and Rules* in this journal, Vol. 21, No. 85, October 1971.

choose the order of these ablutions. At the other end of the scale the point of an ascription of freedom could be very general, thus we can say that in Samoa people are left almost complete sexual freedom. We can also use a remark about freedom in order to contrast different set-ups in a most general way. For example, the anarchists want a "system" which leaves everybody the freedom to do anything. The only sense of "freedom" relevant here is of course social or communal, other senses are to be disregarded. For example where a man is said to have regained his freedom of movement after infantile paralysis, or where a "loss of freedom" occurs when one is forcibly restrained in the absence of any rules at all.

It should be noted that on this level it is possible to be left a freedom, in the sense of not being required to do something, and yet others might restrict us by their actions, robbing us of the benefit of this lack of control. In the absence of actual control their actions are free as well, and can be directed against us, without contravening any rules.

H.J. McCloskey in saying "I am legally entitled under our legal system to do whatever is not forbidden by the law"[10], clearly believes himself to be referring to rights. Thus he does not distinguish between the possession of a right and having a freedom to do something left to one.

This is clearly a consequence of having defined rights as entitlements pure and simple, whereas, as will emerge from subsequent discussions, they are better characterised as *guaranteed* entitlements. McCloskey treats a right as an entitlement to do something and to have the respective act recognised, but does not explain his terms any further. It will be clear that both entitlement and recognition cannot be treated as samples and are easily explained by reference to standing arrangements and rules as discussed above. When this is done the recognition or the entitlement is seen to be guaranteed in terms of some rules, and the need for such a guarantee where a right is concerned is clearly seen.

(c) A rule might *guarantee* one the enjoyment of a certain good – a freedom, the possession or accessibility of something, etc. From the beneficiary's point of view, the position created by this is the *possession of a right.* This is more complex than the leaving of a freedom for now not only there is no bar to X doing *a*, but X can be sure that there will be no bar to his doing *a*, as long as the situation continues.[11]

[10] H. J. McCloskey, "Rights," *Philosophical Quarterly*, 1965.

[11] Cf. here W. N. Hohfeld, (ed.) W. W. Cook, *Fundamental Legal Conceptions as Applied in Judicial Reasoning and other Legal Essays.* Hohfeld distinguishes: Rights, privileges, powers

In keeping with McCloskey's usage but contrary to his position, it might be said that now X is entitled to do *a*, whereas previously he was simply not prevented from doing it.

In order to avoid oversimplifications leading to falsehood as such, the view that "without the possibility of the correlative duty resting somewhere the attribution of the right to X would be meaningless,"[12] three distinctions should be drawn. For clarity's sake, I would like to insist that what is here indicated are different kinds of rights not different concepts of them.

First distinction: one can have a right *against rules* or a right *against people.*

Lack of rules amounts to no guarantee, for the freedom predicated upon it can be taken away at any moment for any reason. If only a rule, or a cluster of rules exist, more cannot be achieved. But since in a code we have a system of rules implementing a policy, it might be *against the understood policy of the code* to have rules dealing with certain kinds of behaviour. The concept is that of it not being proper for the code to have a given rule X. This idea in itself is not novel as will be seen by comparing it with Hohfeld's privilege: "A privilege is the opposite of a duty, and the correlative of a 'no-right' ... the privilege of entering is the negotation of a duty to stay off."[13] The important feature here is that the privilege is against a code or system of rules, and it is the code that lacks the capacity rather than an individual who has a no-right.

In practice a capacity of a code is often limited by a constitutional rule — a meta-rule in this context. In other circumstances such "policy" might be implicit in the code itself, or it might be made explicit in some such words as "it is part of the aim of the code to leave the children to their own devices in finding their ways out of mild stress situations"; alternatively it might be prescribed by a maxim, for example: "expressions of love should be prescribed but left to the discretion of the parties involved."

These are some of the ways of putting a limit on what rules can do,

and immunities (*vide* e.g. p. 6, Introduction by W. W. Cook). All these are rights in the present usage.

[12] S. I. Benn & R. S. Peters, *Social Principles and the Democratic State*, Allen & Unwin, 1959, p. 88. Also *vide* Hohfeld, *op. cit.*, p. 38. "What clue do we find in ordinary legal discourse towards limiting the word in question ('right') to a definite and appropriate meaning? That clue lies in the correlative 'duty,' for it is certain that even those who use the word and the conception 'right' in the broadest possible way are accustomed to thinking of 'duty' as the inevitable correlative."

[13] *Op. cit.*, p. 38–9.

or more exactly, determining what rules are acceptable or proper. The force of the restriction is based on the inconsistency of accepting a given maxim while instituting a contrary rule. This is the clearest example of a right that does not create any duty in others, contrary to the dictum that to every right there must be a corresponding duty. For to infringe a right is not to render it void, so private intrusions in the area are irrelevant, being merely infringements of people's freedom, not an infringement of their right not to have a law dealing with the matter. Parliamentarians do not have a duty to refrain from passing such a law – usually there are no sanctions and rules preventing this and quite obviously such sanctions need not exist. But in the terms of the example, if passed, such a law would be null and void for it would be unconstitutional, or in some comparable way contrary to a valid meta-rule. The court that declares this to be the case has no specific duty to declare it void, it merely has a duty to interpret constitutional rules correctly. If the government acts as if the law was valid it contravenes its duty to act within the law. It could be said marginally that, after the declaration by the court the government has a duty of refraining from enforcing the defunct law, but this is hardly to be consigned *the* specific duty corresponding to *this* right against the rules.

Maxims prescribing as policy that some areas should be left free from rule interference create rights against the rules.[14] In such cases, though free from interference by the rules, one need not be free from all interference. An example that comes to mind is this: according to our moral code, or code of manners, one has the right to be pompous; nor are there any rules in existence saying that others must suffer pompous displays patiently. Thus people have the right to try to stop people from acting pompously. It is an understood policy that both displays of and opposition to displays of pomposity should not be a matter of regulation.

In the above example inter-personal relations came in only because standing arrangements are grounded in them. However, in the case of rights against people, inter-personal relations become in one way or another the prime concern of the arrangements in question. Let us consider four examples of rights against people:

Example a: A wife is thought to have *a right to maintenance*. This right is *against her husband*, it is established by rules, but rules alone are

[14] The terminology is not meant descriptively.

insufficient to carry it – rules cannot provide for a woman, people have to, and in this case her husband is required to do so.

Example b: A wife is thought to have *a right not to be beaten* by her spouse. Here again rules (or a rule) establish the right, but it would be null and void unless it created an obligation in her husband – rules alone cannot carry it.

Example c: People are thought to have *a right to life*, in the sense that others are not permitted to deprive them of it. Here again unless the rule is prescribed for others its effect would be void.[15]

Example d: People are sometimes thought to have *a right to reasonable medical care;* this rule in itself does not involve any particular person in a duty to treat them, or to pay for their doctors, but it creates a social duty of provision of adequate health facilities. Thus it involves other people albeit in a vague way. It is quite sophisticated in that it presupposes complex social structure, but assuming it, the case is clearly intelligible

All these rights implicate other people in a deeper and more direct way than a right against the rules would – for instance, it is inconceivable that anyone should have the right to, or even be free to, interfere with one's exercise of such a right, in contra-distinction to the right to pompous behaviour quoted above.

In the cases *c* and *d* as in the legal case of rights *in rem* there is no specific person charged with a specific duty correlative to the right in question. Hohfeld holds that in such a case we have a cluster of individual duties, rather than a single collective duty corresponding to the right. He says "... the same considerations and tests seem applicable to A's respective rights *in rem*, or multiple rights against B, C, D, and others indefinitely that they respectively considered shall not enter Blackacre. It is not the case of one *joint* duty of the *same* content resting on all."[16] Subsequent discussion makes any such definite view implausible, for in the cases envisaged below we would have to stretch the interpretation to include potential duties in potential situations which could not be specified in advance with any reliability.

Second distinction: It is possible to distinguish between *rights to enjoyment* and *rights to provision.*

[15] McCloskey (*op. cit.*, p. 118 ff.) argues the opposite, but even he must admit that people have no right to deprive others of life – such a lack might seem equivalent to a general duty to respect the life of others.

[16] *Op. cit.*, p. 93–4.

"Enjoyment" is to be understood in the legalistic sense where it means no more than undisturbed possession, or use. A right to enjoyment consists then in being safe from interference but it does not mean that steps will be taken to ensure the right holders continued possession of the specified good.

Examples (b) and (c) above are examples of rights to enjoyment. Examples (a) and (d) are examples of rights to provision. Example (a) involves a specific person, *viz.* the husband, in a duty to provide the maintenance. Clearly such rights can be held against institutions or bodies of men as well as for example a worker's right to his wages, and/or his holidays. Example (d) does not involve any specific performance (as a duty) on the part of any specific person, but it imposes a social requirement for provision of facilities, and if necessary a policy requiring health-restoring actions, on the part of appropriate bodies. Clearly, it is not always possible to say who has or might acquire what duty if this end is to be achieved.

There can be no rights to provision against rules, for *rules cannot provide goods,* though they might compel people to do so. Rules can only determine what should be done, but they are not agents themselves.

The third distinction is between *general* and *specific* rights.

Examples (a) and (b) above are examples of *specific rights.* They are directed at a specifiable person of whom a specific performance is required, or on whose performance there is placed a specific limit, e.g. he has to pay a sum of money weekly. The second is designed to prevent a specific kind of malady, it prevents a particular kind of act. For instance a husband is not thereby prevented from causing his wife pain, anguish and unhappiness by other means. A similar right can be held against an institution or body of men.

Examples (c) and (d) above are examples of *general rights.* Neither of them creates a *specific duty* in anyone. In case (c) a limit is placed on actions of others in a general manner; it does not specify the kind of action to be abstained from, only the kind of effect to be avoided. In this it resembles a policy, which prescribes an end but not the means to it.

Both specific and general rights against rules are possible. *Habeas corpus,* an example of a specific right, is designed to prevent a particular malady, that of anybody having the power to imprison a citizen not shown guilty of a grave offence. The *right to liberty* is general in that it imposes a limit on legislative actions by the way of a maxim "Freedom of Citizens is to be safeguarded". It is not only the case that many legislative decisions of various kinds could contravene this maxim, but also that the freedom itself, unlike avoidance of unlawful arrest, can take an indefinite number of forms, thus it will often be a matter of judgement, whether liberty is in danger, whereas it is not usually a matter of judgement whether someone is arrested and/or placed in prison without a due process of law.

It could be objected that general rights to provision such as an entitlement to reasonable medical care and/or standard of living must create respective specific duties in, for example, the government. This is mistaken. For instance free enterprise governments do not provide all or the majority of goods that are necessary to maintain the minimum level of well-being to which their citizens are thought to be entitled like e.g. the socialist governments attempt to do. This is the case simply because many of the essential goods are provided by private citizens who have no duty to supply public needs. Such duties are ascribed only to public bodies, but these, in terms of the system, are not required to provide e.g. the manufactured goods many of which are indispensable. Now clearly if the citizens in a free enterprise community are deemed to have the right to a standard of living which depends on goods a, b, c, . . . privately produced, there is no one who has the duty to provide the said goods, and consequently it would be difficult to maintain the right creates a respective duty of provision.

It was objected to this point[17] that to say in such circumstances that citizens "have a right" to a decent standard of living is a misleading way of saying that it would be a good thing if people had this right, but that such a right does not in fact exist.

Despite the initial plausibility of this retort the argument seems unconvincing. For instance where wages are fixed by arbitration as e.g. in Australia, such a right is often successfully quoted in a claim for a better wage. Yet the standard of living does not depend on the wage alone – it depends also on prices and on availability of goods. There is in this instance no specific duty requiring the government to ensure these conditions. The arbitration court duly fixes *a fair wage*, and it is left to the discretion of the court what this means. However if what is regarded as a decent standard of living became inaccessible on a

[17] By J. Plamenatz, although his argument was directed more precisely against the view that no duty of any kind, rather than that no specific duty, need correspond to such a right.

large scale the government would be regarded as not only unsuccessful, but as defaulting its mandate – especially if attainment of this goal was possible. This point is not seriously challenged from any side of the political spectrum.

I think that to say in these circumstances that it is the government's duty to provide decent living standards is to say too much. Clearly if it became obvious that only Government action can ensure this such a duty would almost certainly come into existence, which is not to say that it is in existence now. On the other hand to say that citizens have no right to a decent standard of living is to say too little, for the concept of such protected entitlement informs much of the communal thinking.

It would be possible to say here that there is a dormant duty, a duty in abeyance since it requires no action in present circumstances, but this is not correct. Should circumstances deteriorate, the community would be faced with the issue whether to retain the communal expectation that everyone is entitled to a certain standard of living, or to change other rules to do two things to wit either (i) to impose a corresponding duty on say the government, and give the government the necessary powers and rights to achieve this, for clearly it does not possess them now, or (ii) to abandon the expectation and let the other arrangements be. As of present, such a decision is not necessary. It could be objected that the explanation of rights in terms of rules and ultimately of the acceptance of expectations *as positive reasons for acting* precludes the acceptance of a rule where no action is demanded and *a fortiori* the acceptance of the above account. But this is not the case. It is quite possible to have an expectation, to think of it as a positive reason for action, and to leave it completely vague who should act in the belief that as long as somebody is going to do enough the expectation will be fulfilled. As long as it is fulfilled no more is needed, and in particular it is not necessary to specify who should do what in order to fulfil the expectation. But it should be noted that such an attitude is only possible with respect of a maxim, never with respect of a rule, i.e. only where a policy is prescribed, not where a specific act is.

So far we have concentrated on straightforward examples and cases, and this is as it should be. For it is unreasonable to look for the basic features among the complex, controversial or unclear cases. These are almost certain to mislead, and should be put aside till a clear-cut picture emerges. Where such clear cases are concerned the above distinctions clearly establish a reasonably precise picture of the kinds of guarantee that can be provided by rules, and seem to give a reasonable account of rights.

However in complex cases the story might be less straightforward and difficulties of varying seriousness arise. With respect to the present discussion unrecognised rights and unrecognised duties present what might be termed a principal difficulty, and it is with a discussion of these that it must end.

It seems to make sense to say that for instance Roman slaves had a right to liberty, yet, it was not recognized by anybody in Rome, perhaps not in the whole ancient world, including the slaves themselves. Of course there are also the well-known general duties complementary to unrecognised rights. Thus there arises the unrecognised general duty of all Romans to respect the lives of all, including the lives of their slaves, which duty might be the subject of an analogous difficulty.

Since both duties and rights were defined in terms of rules, and these in turn in terms of standing arrangements, there seems to be no room in the present account for completely unrecognised rights, duties and/ or freedoms. Up to a certain point seemingly unrecognised duties and rights can be accommodated directly, and in other cases remarks of this kind can make sense, but are seen to have a special character.

An obvious case of an unrecognised duty is provided by a conscientious objector who not only fails to accept the arrangement by which he has the e.g. military duty, but is opposed to any form of activity of the relevant kind for anybody at all anywhere and at any time. It would seem unreasonable to claim that he accepts the standing arrangements responsible for the duty to which he objects. The question then becomes: can a duty be imposed on the unwilling subject? The answer is patently "yes" – not all duties are the effect of voluntary subjection. We might also point out that if this was not so unrecognised rights correlative of duties could not exist in any case. How then is such an imposition of duty possible? The most obvious and common case is one where the duty in question though not directly solicited is a consequence of the carrying out of arrangements which have been accepted. Thus acceptance of the rule of the law, as passed by the parliament and promulgated by the government, might imply the acceptance of unpopular and unwanted duties arising out of laws duly passed and promulgated, that *in consistency* must be followed. This seems even more reasonable since it is understood in most cases that no one decision is likely to satisfy everybody, indeed it is this that makes, as Hobbes saw, the institution of government essential, which is not to say that freedoms or channels for raising objections to decisions cannot be provided in the system. It would be naive to present this as the answer to all problems. The point has also a practical limit for if sufficient numbers of laws are obnoxious, respect for parliament and law become defunct. Nor will this deal with the conscientious objector who reserves to himself and others the right to object to an occasional rule.

But on this model one can justify impositions of many unwanted restrictions. In fact as long as they arise as the result of routine working of the usual arrangements we are *not forced* to allow any expectations. No agreement can be reliable if it leaves people freedom to renounce it at will, and reliability is the point of communal arrangements. Thus these arrangements have a tendency to be self-perpetuating.

It seems possible for an individual, say a conscientious objector, to get out of this kind of dilemma by renouncing the whole package deal, and then his position as a conscientious objector becomes impregnable but carries with it unpleasant consequences. For to renounce the package deal is to disclaim its benefits as much as its duties and impositions.[18] We are so much entrenched in a communal style of life that we would find it difficult to imagine what it would be like to give it up – complete anarchy is a state of affairs that few want and fewer can visualize.

This point is not to be taken as showing that the society's rules have an absolute authority over its members – it is in fact reasonable to resist them actively if this might bring about a desired and/or urgent change without causing too much damage to communal structure – this testing and forging of arrangements in action is the oldest, most basic and a very common method of social engineering. But the above points show what sort of hold communal rules can have over unwilling members of the group, and what grounds can be advanced for enforcing them. If we reach the limit these are in terms of internal consistency of the arrangements in question, and are formally unanswerable.

In the nature of the case the reason against enforcement must be more broadly based and concerned with what the arrangements should be, which is not to say that such reasons cannot be advanced in favour of the *status quo*, as well.

It would be a mistake to suppose that all communal arrangements are explicit and that their actual force rests on their formal features,

[18] Such a unilateral declaration need not of course deprive the person in question of these communal benefits.

such as the consistency point raised above. It is enough for people to feel obliged to do some things and to feel assured that others will do them as well. Community depends on the actual actions of people, as well as on such assurance. If people were to refuse to take arrangements, and their consequences, seriously, no community could arise at all and in a drastic case no co-operation either. But even when the community and its rules are accepted, such acceptance is unlikely to be either single-minded or absolute. Most of us have quite a few reservations about most of them, but the reservations are generally less important than the arrangement as a whole. Some people would engage in disastrous non-conformity, but then others are unlikely to permit them to do so.

The question might be raised whether they have any right to do so. I have tried to argue that a reasonable amount of necessary conformity must be in consistency accepted along with the acceptance of communal life, but this is not an argument for enforcing this or that particular obedience. How to apply the general maxim to particular cases is a matter of judgment but the point of consistency is important – thus it seems reasonable to allow people the freedom to go into a retreat in the desert to do what they please, but in the middle of a city one may do less of what one pleases. If someone wants to do away with *all social arrangements*, this creates a different problem – others have sufficient reason to restrain him, do they have the right? In terms of communal arrangements the question cannot arise, for on the basis of what could the anarchist claim the right to freedom from interference? Similarly *vice versa*. In practice, pragmatic reasons are usually the strongest: does this individual's behaviour constitute a danger to the style of life, security, etc. of the conventionalist others? If it does he should be restrained for the sake of those in danger. It is primitive to regard every non-conformity as a threat, and it is less of a threat the more sophisticated and complex the society. On the other hand it is a folly to regard every rebellious act as unimportant. Between the Scylla of the one and the Charybdis of the other common sense, experience, and science might help to steer a middle course. It is a democratic and a pluralist attitude to allow as much dissent as is compatible with stability, but it is not the only attitude possible.

For instance it might be claimed that it is immoral to coerce an anarchist, or to coerce a conscience. This would be normally regarded as relevant, for it cannot be regarded as desirable to exert immoral pressures. If such a decision is accepted in the face of good reasons to the contrary, a price must be paid for avoiding the morally dubious. The price might be too high, and it might be less moral to pay the price than to over-rule the original point.

It will be clear from the above that (a) in a strict sense duties unrecognised by the participants can be imposed upon them, and (b) that there might be various good reasons which might suffice to regard such imposition as wrong or unreasonable.

This deals with the relatively simple problem of the lack of recognition of an otherwise existing duty by some individuals. A comparatively simple form of an unrecognised right will arise when for instance in terms of the existing rules one has a right without realising it, and without others realising it. Law recognises this for it makes provisions for settling points of law, as well as points of fact – and the former concerns the position created by legal rules. These points have to be settled, can be discovered and are often a matter of controversy. Thus the matter is so far easily settled in principle but this will not do for the real problem where it is clear that legal, communal rules, etc. make no provision for such rights, and yet one wishes to claim that the right exists unrecognised. This was the difficulty illustrated by the case of the supposed right to life vested in Roman slaves.

How could it be claimed that Roman slaves had the "unrecognised" right to liberty or their masters the unrecognised general duty to respect their liberty in the absence of any communal rules establishing those? The simple answer that need not detain us long is in terms of some other kind of principles, the favourite being moral or those ordained by God. This solution might lead to many a problem if implemented in detail, but is clear-cut in principle for it establishes that right or duty in terms of discernible rules, and namely the rules of God, the moral rules, etc. etc. Since it is possible to claim unrecognised rights with respect to any set of rules the problem is not solved in principle.

The only plausible interpretation of this by no means unpopular way of talking is to take it that the point of asserting an existence of an unrecognised right is to stress the claimant's opinion that such a right *should be given*. Thus the subject of the Spanish Inquisition did not have, but should have had, the right to abandon his religion, his belief in God, etc.

The point of making the strictly speaking incorrect claim that a right actually *exists* is emphasis. The point is that the claimant purports to accept a maxim *viz.* a general rule, in terms of which there is such a right, and the "right" is thereby forcibly stressed. The speaker assumes it exerts pressure on others to accept this maxim, and claims by implication that if any existing code is at variance with this maxim the code should be suitably amended.[19] It could be perhaps best described by saying that the claimant announces an expectation, and by implication claims it to be communal or moral.

There could be the best of reasons to support this kind of point, e.g. they could be moral, and compelling, as in the case of a right not to be tortured in order to provide sadistic pleasure to others. In this case the moral reasons are so strong and so obvious that there is hardly any need to state them, and hardly any need to list any such precise right in our books.[20] In another type of case the maxim in terms of which the envisaged right would exist is held, and sometimes held rightly, to be essential to the health of the community, to its development, etc. Such might be an envisaged right to education.

Since in these terms the "existence" of even totally unrecognised rights and duties is easily intelligible within the framework developed above, their existence cannot be regarded as an objection to the system.

[19] Cf. here C. L. Stevenson, *Ethics and Language*, Yale University Press, 1945, especially Chapter II.

My point is that the claim that a totally unrecognised right exists is emotive, and can be analysed on Stevenson's lines.

[20] Since morality need not be understood in terms of rules this does not contradict the point made above, p. 53 ff.

CHAPTER III

STATUS AND POSITION

With the help of concepts discerned in the first two chapters some quite complex relations between members of the community can be stated. We can describe different types of rules, their different effects, and in these terms we can talk about duties, freedoms, liberties, etc. We could discern different types of rights, different types of freedoms and liberties and so on. We also can give an account of clusters of rules, codes and systems. This is admittedly quite a complex picture. Still it is a flat picture. But it is as yet impossible to treat inequalities with any degree of precision, yet inequality is a necessary element of any sophisticated organization. Though it is quite clear that the effects differentiate between people this was not dealt with directly. To illustrate: if a gentleman ought to give preference to ladies when entering a building, then gentlemen are not treated equally with ladies in terms of this rule. This rule creates a more deep-seated inequality than a rule which says that whoever has worked for four hours is entitled to an hour's break, for everybody *could* be in this position, but not everybody could be in the position of a lady. Also it will be clear that such differences can be very complex and no less important an element of the group structure than rules, codes and systems of codes. Furthermore these differences are complementary to the existence of most of the rules.

Differences of the above kind are status differences. We can say that: *Two people are different in status with respect to a rule or a set of rules if it is the case that the same rule or set of rules gives different guarantees, allows different freedoms, or places different obligations on the two people.* Thus if the rule says whenever A requests something, B is to fulfil the request, but whenever B requests something A is to fulfil the request if and only if he feels so inclined, then there is a difference in status between A and B with respect to this rule. Differences of status can of course arise with respect to a rule, with respect to a cluster of rules, with respect to a code or a system of codes, etc.

If there is a rule such that some people have a different status with respect to it, and another rule supports this one, and still another which limits the two rules previously mentioned, then the status of a person, with respect to the first rule, will be significant with respect to the second and third as well, and will be affected by them. For example, the privileged position of ladies with respect to the code of manners will have to be maintained by any regulation belonging to the code, especially if the status difference was the point of the arrangements. Now if we have a regulation that limits, say, the two previous regulations, such as an emergency regulation, it might either preserve the difference of treatment, so preserving the difference in status as for instance emergency regulations for sinking ships give preference to women and children, or it might disregard it. Thus, if we take regulations for using fire escapes when a fire threatens, it might very well be specified that people should leave at the nearest possible exit in order of their proximity without waiting for the ladies to come first, thus limiting the scope of the code of manners and abandoning the status difference in this case. Whenever rules are related to each other, and a rule involves status differences, then these differences may, and very often will be involved in systematic relations between this and other rules. If we have a code, then significant status differences will tend to be differences in terms of the code rather than in terms of this or that particular rule. Look at the football field: the umpire, the centre-forward, the coach, those are status descriptions. Given a football code we might maintain that the difference between an umpire and a centre-forward is manifested in this particular rule, that a difference between a centre-forward and a follower is manifested in that particular rule, that the difference between a coach and an umpire is manifested in this rule and so on. But it is quite clear that if you said no more than that you would have said something very misleading, for it is the entire set of relevant rules which really determines status differences between those people.

The types of cases where an unchangeable natural characteristic, like sex, is cited as the basis of status are relatively rare. Much more often one is *selected* to be an umpire or to be a judge, or *places himself in the position* of the accused, or is *placed in the position* of beneficiary, etc. This gives rise to the question: What then determines a person's status in these cases and why should he bear this rather than that status?

What kind of status it is is determined by the rules involved – it is they that specify what are the duties, prerogatives, etc. of e.g.: judge, counsel, witnesses, plaintiff, etc. at court – they spell out the exact position in which those enjoying, or suffering, a given status are.

But we do not turn to such rules to *find what status we suffer or enjoy.* This comes about in a different way – a judge is appointed, the counsel engaged, the accused charged, etc. Thus the fact that one finds oneself in this, that or another status position can be determined in different ways in different cases.

The next nearest to our example of a rule appertaining to someone because of a natural characteristic such as sex or being a typhoid carrier, is found where one places oneself in a status position by one's own actions *significant in terms of the rules concerned.*

Significantly for the subsequent discussion, status is determined by a number of rules when they form an organised set of rules.[1] Such a set is likely to be a package deal just like a code, though it might fail to be a code if it is e.g. limited to status creating considerations only. The rules in such a set usually support each other in determining the status of an individual or more appropriately individuals. For example the accused in a court *may* have his liberty taken away either during or as a result of the proceedings, he *can* engage counsel, he *cannot* be treated as guilty unless convicted, he has the right to refuse to incriminate himself, etc.

It will be seen that more than one rule is needed to create a status difference for a rule can only be obeyed or disobeyed and this does not leave enough scope to create a status difference.[2] Thus if we have a rule saying (i) "bow to a lady," it only states what to do if one meets a lady; this alone cannot even determine whether men or women should obey this directive – whoever has internalised the rule obeys it. But if we add another regulation: (ii) "Gentlemen are to obey the rule 'Bow to a lady", this is more promising; it looks like creating a standing difference between men and women. Now add a third and fourth regulation: (iii) "Ladies are to obey the regulation (iv) 'One does not bow to a gentleman'" and we have a much more impressive position: "lady" and "gentleman" are now status concepts for they have a different position with respect to the rules and each other.

This is of course only a rudimentary status, but the point of the example was to illustrate the opposite, to wit, that one regulation on its own cannot create an effective status difference.

One would of course come to a different conclusion if one were to

[1] Here status seems a counterpart of a policy *vis-à-vis* persons.

[2] *Vide* above, Chapter I, p. 23–4.

think of a rule as more complex, e.g. R.M. Dworkin[3] says: "The United States Constitution with all its difficulties of interpretation may be considered a single rule of interpretation". It might be best to distinguish between simple and complex rules, as well as between regulations and maxims. If so, I am at the moment referring to simple rules. A complex rule could consist of all the simple rules (i) to (iv) taken together. This would be a complex regulation, but a complex maxim is also possible. Returning to the point at issue, the rule(s) quoted above will amount to the acquiring of a special status provided only that two other conditions are satisfied: (a) that the range of the cluster of relevant duties etc. so acquired is wide enough to justify this name, and (b) that the consequences appertaining to *X*'ing are standing and can be expressed in rules.[4]

We could put this by saying that status can be acquired by *X*'ing, if there is a rule *R* such that in terms of *R*, *X*'ing makes one subject to further rules $r^1, r^2, r^3, \ldots r^n$, which together form a cluster offering a wide enough range of rights, duties and freedoms. When status is conferred by others, as for instance in the cases of: an election, an appointment, etc., the situation is more complex for it might involve a cluster of different actions by different people to *X* and to invoke *R*, but the basic principle is unaltered. An action or actions specified in rule R takes place, and in terms of R has status-conferring consequences. A status appellation such as: a criminal, a married man, etc., is often given to anyone who *X*'es (or is *X*'ed) provided only that *X*'ing carries with it a set of consequences that are sufficient to create the status position thus named.

Status is not merely a position *vis-à-vis* a code, or system in which one can find oneself, but a *standing position*. Thus it is almost sufficient to relate status to rules, codes, etc. since these are standing arrangements, but not quite sufficient since they can and do permit *ad hoc* arrangements. The standing position is determined in terms of the arrangements significant within the scope of the code, system, institution or community in question, and it is determined in a relatively permanent way. There is of course quite a wide scope of possible arrangements with status import. Let us just list: the status of an accused – suffered with respect to the system of law enforcement and typically carried

[3] R. M. Dworkin, *Is Law a System of Rules?*, 35, University of Chicago Legal Review, 1967, also in R. S. Summers (ed.), *Essays in Legal Philosophy*, Blackwell, 1967.

[4] It would be possible to construe "status" in such a way that all such differences would be included in it, but this does not seem advisable, and is out of step with the main use of the word in ordinary parlance.

over to this, that or another court convened for this, that or another proceeding; the status of a citizen – with respect to the community – a more stable position than the previous one and significant over a far wider range of arrangements.

Need status acquired with respect to one code be involved in another which supports it? It may and it may not. The Superintendent of the Police Force may have special status with respect to the traffic code, yet while the law concerning assault and battery may place limitations upon the football code the status difference between a centre-forward and a coach will be unaffected by this. Thus status might be limited to one code or may transgress codes. A status difference could be conceivably defined by just one simple rule. Admittedly this is a limiting case of the application of the concept. Examples that come to mind are: "Women and children first," or "Always obey the generalissimo."

The above is not precise or definite enough to decide status questions by simple application of the description offered. There will be many twilight zones where there is need for judgment. However it is clear that rules differentiate between people, that these differences carry over to codes and systems of codes, and that differences with sufficient range to carry status will easily arise. It is also clear that if we were to insist on absolute status equality we would preclude any significant sophistication of the rule structure of the community from occurring. For then the following type of rules would be barred: Judges and only judges can pass sentence and adjourn courts; Officers must be obeyed; Garbage collectors *qua* garbage collectors should call for garbage at least twice a week, etc. In the absence of status differences we would have to delete all positions such as: officer, judge, accused, garbage collector, etc., etc., making division of labour unworkable if not impossible.[5]

The concept of status and the possibility of inequality in such terms is immensely important. Everywhere where specialization is needed, there must be those who direct, and if the performance is at all complex those who carry out this; those who carry out that; and those who carry out the other part of the plan. Now this could be *ad hoc*, if the set-up is concerned with achieving a particular end. But if it is a part of the standing way in which the community is organized, then it results in status differences – those people are judges; those policemen; those brokers; etc. This then makes it possible to have a much more sophisticated structure of the community, it can now include varie-

[5] It should be remembered here that rules as here defined can be tacit – so that tacit division of tasks is also precluded by the dictum contemplated.

gated teams, institutions and organizations, and, of course, since there can be rules dealing with these as well – institutions, etc., can now have different relative standing such as where for instance the supreme court has jurisdiction over the doings of commercial, public and political bodies. The importance of status lies basically in this opening up of a new dimension in communal structure and communal engineering.

Let us observe that *A*'s status with respect to a code, institution, system, etc., might have ramifications for *A*'s status with respect to another code, etc., and thus have a wider significance. A general status, not obviously tied to any definite code, set or institution, is also possible. Examples will be provided by: a sage; a charity worker; a person who is always asked to organize charity drives, etc. *A* might be always asked to be an organizer because in every case he appears to be the best candidate. But this need not be so – it might be the done thing to ask Smith to be a secretary and if one were to propose Brown one might get the reply: "But surely we cannot omit Smith, can we?". In such case Smith has a *de facto* status that could be expressed in the maxim: "Ask Smith first to be a secretary if you need one,"relating to a standing arrangement that he is to be favoured. On this model a community can involve the existence of implicit or explicit status differentiating rules in its own right. Such "communal status" can be limited to a certain section of the community – for example J. Doe is always asked to represent the charitable organizations by religious people; it can be limited to a certain kind of thing – for example R. Roe is always asked to organize things; or it can be relatively unlimited – for example old Blimp is always in everything that is going on.

It is easily seen why, as was remarked above, status adds another and important dimension to the forms of communal structure. The new set-up makes it possible to use people's special talents better. Tasks can be allotted (a) on a standing basis or (b) *ad hoc* by people whose status entitles them to allot tasks and to supervise the carrying out of this decision etc. Thus the social machinery can become more adaptable and better suited for dealing with a variety of tasks, some of which are unforeseeable. To say all this is to say only that emergence of status involves this sophistication, and add, not to comment on the actual development of communal forms. In practice forms of a different type could easily arise together.

The concepts of: "status", "rule," "effect of a rule," etc. are complementary to each other. Rules determine in terms of their effects the status of those to whom they apply. One's status expresses one's standing *vis-à-vis* the rules that apply to him, either totally or with respect to a certain set of rules.[6] Rules are more basic than status, for we understand status in terms of rules, not *vice versa*. One could maintain plausibly that the existence of one rule, having only one effect, would not justify status differentiations. Status differences are thus seen to presuppose a certain minimum level of sophistication. But it should be noted that a more primitive level could easily never be instantiated in actual practice.

Status differences are inequalities which often are administratively and/or structurally both necessary and desirable. And yet it is traditional to regard equality as desirable, and the opposite as reprehensible. People like Rousseau have been prompted to develop whole political theories in order to show how equality could be preserved. It is unlikely that they could have meant by equality the undesirable, unsophisticated, primitive state which I have envisaged above, i.e. they used the term more narrowly than I have defined it for the present purpose.[7]

The traditional demand might be a demand for justice, where unjust inequalities are condemned, but this will not quite do, because the demand for equality can be seen as an attempt to explain what social justice consists in.

Let us envisage two sets of rules regarding Sergeants in the Army who:

according to Type A:	*according to Type B:*
can give orders to privates;	get better medical treatment;
decide what is to be done;	get better food than do privates;
are to be obeyed by privates;	can use privates for personal services;
etc.	etc.

To object against inequality is not to object to set *A*, but to object to set *B* of the rules. This ought to suggest to us that equality is here to be understood in terms of fairness, for *necessary and unavoidable inequality is seen to be acceptable*. The demand is in effect for avoidance of unnecessary inequality.

The first question arising here is what inequality is worrying *per se*, and it is clear that it is worrying only if it puts some people at a dis-

[6] The case where all the rules apply equally to everyone might be regarded as a limited case of status *viz.* where everyone has equal status e.g. that of a citizen.

[7] Actually Rousseau dit not dream of preserving absolute equality, but only what could be termed political equality.

advantage *vis-à-vis* others. The second and main question is what inequality is necessary; what unnecessary?[8] I think that it must be answered first of all in structural terms. Take for instance the Country Fire Authority. Now it is the business of the organization to deal promptly and effectively with fires. It consists of a number of individuals spread over a reasonably wide area. Unless someone had the status conferring on him the authority to direct the actions of others to tell them where to go and what to do, the objectives of this organization would be thwarted – so this inequality, i.e. between leader and the led, is necessary – but the efficiency of the organization does not depend on e.g. the leader being able to demand better food, better clothing, or more votes in the next election, than the rank and file members. This last inequality is then unjustified on the pragmatic and structural ground.

The application of this principle in practice can cause difficulties. E.g. should accountants get better pay than clerks, should officers be entitled to be addressed as *sir* by lesser ranks – are those privileges or pragmatic needs? – clearly arguments can be advanced on both sides of the dispute. The precise scope of such inequalities, if they are accepted in principle, might be even more difficult to agree upon. On the other hand structural and practical efficiency is not the only desideratum. No one wishes for a 1984 type of community – so perhaps if the inequalities demanded are too great, the price should not be paid. Slavery comes to mind as an example – it might have been true that slavery was economically the best method in Ancient Rome and in relatively recent America, it might even be best and cheapest in a contemporary state, e.g. South Africa – if this is a fact, we need not agree that the inequalities involved in slave ownership are thereby justified.

The unequal treatment in terms of rules and at least some of the problems that arise in this area need some further attention.

A and *B* receive different treatment if in terms of the same regulations person *A* has different duties, freedoms and rights from person *B*. At least on one point what the one person is enjoined to do, or what that person is permitted to do, or what that person is guaranteed must not be required, permitted or guaranteed to the other person. The first problem is how can it be determined which person has the (a) status and which the (b) status? In order to do this it will be necessary to

[8] Cf. here A. M. Honoré, "Social Justice," 8, *McGill Law Journal*, 78, 1962, and revised version in *Essays in Legal Philosophy*. His two principles relate to the two questions asked here.

establish three points, and namely: *the class of people to whom the regulation applies in one way; the class of people to whom the regulation applies in the other way; and the scope of the regulation*, that is, the overall class of people to whom the regulations can apply in one way or another. Some difficulty might be created by the fact that the scope of a regulation or code cannot be determined by the regulation or code itself. This point will be argued more fully later on. The immediate problem lies in understanding how regulations can apply to two different classes of people in different ways if those are not natural classes.

Actual examples are plentiful. Judges are not a different natural class from counsel, or defendants. Government members, and private public are not different natural classes. Nowadays, it will be generally agreed that these and e.g. the differences between the King and his subjects are established by convention, that is, more precisely, by regulations and procedures which set up and control communal organization. It would seem that status differences can exist if and only if people are treated differently by the relevant rules, and on the other hand, that people can be treated differently by the relevant rules if and only if they are referred to in those rules *per* their status and not in their capacity as certain human beings. As has been said before status can be acquired by *X*'ing or by being *X*'ed, the problem is how this can be achieved efficiently in reasonably complex cases, and whether *X*'ing is the only way possible.

There are two main ways out of this problem. It is possible to have a provision for *declaring* people to belong to this, that or another status group. This happens for instance when a number of young boys want to play football; they do not fall into two natural groups which form natural teams, but they select the teams in one way or another. Once selected, they are treated as different teams and try to outdo each other in the game. With respect to a code, selection by meta-rules of R-type would seem possible though not necessary. For the code consists of a number of regulations, and the regulations can provide for any contingency that might arise, so they might provide both for treating people in a different way, and for marking them off for such treatment. It is after all possible for persons who are declared to belong to a class (a) by a procedure (b) internal to the code to have to be treated in a (d) way and to have (d) type duties, freedoms and rights. People who by the procedure (c), internal to the code, have to be delegated to group (g) can at the same time be given treatment (s) and (s) type duties, freedoms and rights.

There is an as yet unresolved difficulty in that all the procedures mentioned so far presuppose that we already have the concept of status and status differences. The type of selection specified above amounts to ascribing different explicitly specified statuses to different people. That makes it unfit as a primary method, unless all status differences are bound to natural classes and seen as such in a biologically direct way[9] but this is unlikely. Somewhere, a break must be established between natural differences and differential treatment. It is sensible not to feed strawberries to someone allergic to them. This could be seen as a status difference between him and strawberry eaters. It need not be so regarded, and would be unlikely to be so regarded unless the concept of status was already established. We do not regard dogs and chickens as having a different status, we just think of them as different, and consequently deal with them in different ways. This would be quite adequate to the above situation as well and unless status ascription was already a method of ensuring differential treatment it cannot be expected to arise in this situation and without other factors operating.

Even in cases where a natural difference leads to differential treatment of rules, the concept of status need not arise. To have a concept of status is to have an idea that someone can occupy a special position *vis-à-vis* rules, such that the rules confer on him a certain range of deliberately concerted rights, duties, freedoms, etc. Thus to think of status is to think in terms of a package deal. If this is given – a person of a special kind – e.g. a psychic person, can give rise to the question – what package-deal of special duties, freedoms, rights, etc. is needed to give this person his or her due, or to ensure that the community benefits by his or her ability, etc. Thus the question is asked: "What status is appropriate for this person?". In absence of status concepts, special provisions can be made one by one, resulting in what might appear to us *but not to the participants*, to be a *de facto* conferring of a special status on this person. Thus we still need to see how the concept of status can arise in the first place. To clarify the issue it might be best to look now at a different aspect of the problem.

Clearly people can come to have special status without being regarded as belonging to a different *natural* class. A man no different from anybody else might just happen to become an established leader or adviser. It simply might that he was there longer, as could be the case with

[9] I am indebted for the discussion of this point to Miss L. M. Broughton. The "biologically" qualification is a reference to an interesting view expounded by E. H. Lenneberg in *Biological Foundations of Language*, John Wiley & Son, N.Y., 1967.

the superior status of the old people in primitive societies. As a different example, take two people trying to catch a runaway horse. The man who happens on this occasion to react more quickly says: "We will have to split. You go right and I will go left", and they do so. A number of similar contingencies might arise. If each time the same man *happens* to take the initiative, then he may come to expect the other to do what he tells him to do, and the other can very well accept this. It is a natural development, for the taking of the initiative becomes easier with repetition, and accepting leadership can become a habit. A habit in itself is not a standing arrangement, but the Rubicon can be crossed very easily when a reciprocal expectation and mutual acceptance of these expectations is added to the picture. The emergent relation involves a status distinction of sorts which can be stated as a rule, *viz.* John Doe is to follow the instructions of Richard Roe in all cases of common endeavour.

It might be thought that any standing arrangement involves a status difference for if it is *A*'s wish that is operative *B*'s status is lower with respect to *A*. This is not so, if the wish becomes shared, no one has *his bidding* done in the obvious sense. In the case of communal expectations this becomes very clear; e.g. one is expected to be decent, but there is no one in particular who is responsible for the existence of this expectation. But where Doe is to follow the instructions of Roe, there exists a classical status distinction – Roe and Doe have here different duties and rights: one is to obey, the other to command.

It could be maintained that the first difference can easily be a difference of status for the rule quoted above is a maxim and prescribes a policy in at least one good sense, but the case furnishes a good occasion to qualify some of the previous statements: *Firstly* in this case the demarcation line between a regulation and a maxim becomes strained, for we could justifiably claim that: "Whenever Richard Roe issues an instruction John Doe is to accept it" is a rule dealing with a single contingency. Nonetheless the rule has such a scope that it must be regarded as a policy decision. It seems reasonable to accept the view that we have a maxim, for the description of the so-called single contingency is very general, and covers a range of actually very different possibilities, however we are reminded that the picture is not clear-cut; *Secondly*, we are reminded that the range required by the "definition" of a status, can be provided in two ways, i.e. by the number or by the scope of the rules in question. In the present situation the scope is paramount, but in most actual cases both should be taken into consideration.

The case discussed above shows only one of the ways in which a status distinction could emerge. One case is sufficient to illustrate the possibility, but to fill in the picture let us consider one other example: *A* is good at tree-climbing but weak, while *B* is strong and good at breaking coconuts, but is poor at climbing. *This is a natural but not a status difference.* In practice, A and B will each drift naturally towards the personally easier task – now if this habit gave rise to appropriate expectations which in turn were accepted as reasons for acting by *A* and *B*, *A* becomes the picker, *B* the breaker of nuts, who perform their tasks *because they are expected to do them.* Now again a status difference, in terms of appropriate rules can be seen to emerge in a natural way between these individuals.

In similar terms an arrangement of this kind could become communal rather than personal, and could get to be incorporated in communal structure resulting in communal status differences. However in the way specified above only personal status can be established, i.e. a kind of arrangement that can concern only John Doe, Joseph Stalin or Charles de Gaulle for it arose with respect to that particular person, and no one else can become Doe, Stalin or de Gaulle. The most useful and interesting status differences however are not tied to personalities and contingencies of communion between them.

The important thing established so far is the possibility of the emergence differences *qua* status differences. There is no need for a prior possession of the concept of status, for the envisaged development to take place, all that is necessary is that individuals should act differently, and then this difference can become enshrined in standing arrangements involving these individuals. Given this the concept of a formalised difference of this kind, i.e. status, can arise, particularly where the difference is communally useful.

There is a problem in that where there are not even subtle differences between individuals with respect to e.g. aptitude for leadership, it might be difficult, if not impossible for *personal status* to arise or its emergence might require the prior possession of an idea of status. This situation though it can be easily enough envisaged is quite unlikely to arise in fact.

The above is not to be understood as a comment on the likely actual developments in a social group. That is an empirical problem not to be solved by pure cogitation. But what was described is possible, and in turn in those terms it is possible to envisage the emergence of status differences. With less than was posited above such an emergence seems to be out of the question. This becomes quite clear when it is remembered that no use can be made of the concept of status before the relevant kind of difference has emerged. In those terms it should be then possible to demonstrate the structural interdependence of various elements of communal organisation.

A regulation which establishes differences between people may arise in a practical situation for practical reasons. Furthermore such a difference could become essential in the group structure. For instance, other regulations can be so framed that they cannot otherwise operate – a simple example: "When you cannot resolve your differences go to Solon for advice." If Solon were to die, the whole structure of the community would collapse or undergo a serious crisis, for in such a case it is tied *ad hoc* to his personal standing. In this way a severe limit is placed on its sophistication and usefulness. But then the status position, or *simply* position, might become part of the *formal* structure if it ceases to be tied to a given person. Usually when this is the case there are rules concerning *replacement of leaders*, etc. (for example, to be succeeded by the eldest son, to be elected, etc.). It is easier to choose a new leader than to change the group structure to suit available personalities. Once existing, *positions* in themselves will be rule dependent, but there must be in the community a conception of *position* as a *standing status difference* prior to this, for the rules creating it must be addressed towards creating a particular status as such. This statement must be somewhat qualified, for it is not necessarily the case that members of the community in question have to be able to say what status is, nor yet need they have a word for status. However there must be enough to make it possible for a status difference to arise as, as it were, a by-product of the regulation structure i.e. it must be possible for the difference to become the direct object of some of the regulations. In these cases there must be awareness of the object of the arrangements made. This implies knowledge of what difference is wanted, but there is no need to think in terms of a "position" as such, for it is possible to think of a position indirectly. For example take a status tied to a natural difference that is not thought of as status. There might arise a wish to preserve the convenience created by the standing achieved by the man Solon, and to replace him when the time comes. A procedure can be devised to ensure finding a suitable substitute. Here a status position as such is set up, even though there is as yet no explicit concept of a status position. Quite clearly the position of e.g. the living Buddha is in fact a rule-created status position, even if it is ostensibly claimed that all the persons holding it are in fact the same person reincarnated. Not all positions could emerge in this indirect way, for while status positions of some kinds could be borne by naturally emerging personalities others could not. It is rare for someone to emerge as an examiner and impossible for the positions of a judge's associate to emerge naturally. The neatest test of whether there is a formal position of a leader, a judge's associate, etc. as such consists in saying that it exists if and only if *the position could fall vacant,* for then it is a part of the structure of the community, and clearly a standing arrangement in its own right.

Such standing status arrangements are determined in terms of duties, rights, prerogatives, etc. In a given community every person becoming e.g. the August Leader will have *the same position.* In the case of natural leadership – each leader could easily have different, though broadly similar, status. In fact even a conventional leader will usually develop an additional nonconventional standing that could make the difference between his being a good or a bad leader. This can be graphically illustrated by the difference in standing between Churchill and Anthony Eden, even though both attained the very same position. Such personal differences grow *ad hoc* and naturally it is only the standing positions, or *status-slots,* that must be developed as such specifically and formally, and it is only where the status-slots are concerned that the participants must be aware of the nature of the difference desired before they can attempt to design the formation-rules needed for its existence. Where only personal standing is in question particular rules can arise independently — each to cover a different aspect of the situation. This might ultimately create an awareness of the fact that these rules taken together have a specific joint effect, but it need not – the position is intelligible without it. Should the concept of status already exist – the development of personal standing could be speeded up and assisted – for the person could be seen as deserving a special status, and given one, but this is a further question.

Unless rules apply identically to all people in the community, those to whom this set of regulations does apply in this way are regarded as different from those to whom it applies in another: for example they are privates rather than officers, and this creates a problem for the difference has to be marked. This arises specifically where status is concerned, for *it* depends on rule-inequality. In a code or in a cluster of regulations, some member regulations may establish the difference between some individuals while others prescribe selective behaviour with regard to them. But in the last resort neither a code nor a regulaction can establish to whom it itself applies. This is a simple matter of logic for, to establish the scope of a code or regulation in a formal manner requires distinguishing between the people to whom it applies and others to whom it does not apply. Clearly a regulation can be general and start with the word "everybody" or particular and start with a word such as "private soldiers". In the second case it does not specify its own scope, for it does not establish who is a private soldier. In the first case it does not do this, for if it is rule in say Outer Mongolia it does not apply to me. In practice the problem need not be visible in such a case for the rule will be obeyed by those who, as we may say, recognize it, but this is a different point. Clearly a regulation (code) is significant only with respect to those to whom it applies. To distinguish between people who are and are not the subject of a regulation it is necessary to specify some individuals as affected by the regulation, and some as not affected. And this is what this very regulation cannot do, because it cannot pronounce about the other people *precisely* because it does not apply to them. Contrary to this it might seem possible for a regulation to specify that certain people are not subject to it. This is misleading because if a regulation says explicitly that some people are not restricted by it, then this regulation *gives them a freedom from restriction.* Yet to say that a rule does not apply to someone is tantamount to saying that he is not just free but independent, that is he need not perform in the manner *required* by this rule, he can disregard it completely. It will be obvious that a freedom can be offered where it could be conceivably restricted:[10] thus when such a freedom is successfully given to some individuals in terms of a given rule or rules, then they are in fact subject to the respective rule, or rules. A description of a situation is not a rule concerning it, and it is not disputed here that a description can be given.

For clarity's sake it is best to agree that a rule can have only one direct effect i.e. that it is simple, and to regard all complex rules as composite i.e. more than one rule even if expressed in a single formula.[11] It is of course always possible for secondary effects to arise. For instance a man given the right to issue orders to everybody else might achieve as the result of this a high status and great snob value, but in terms of the basic rule it would be in order to obey without either agreement or

[10] *Vide* Chapter II, p. 44 ff.

[11] *Vide* R. M. Dworkin, *op. cit.*; also p. 61 above.

respect. Pursuant to this, any claim that a single regulation permits people not to obey it must be wrong, for such a rule would be self-stultifying. In contradistinction, in terms of a cluster or a code there are means for specifying that a regulation or a sub-cluster of regulations does not affect some of the people who then have this freedom *in terms of this code.* Since it is in terms of some of its regulations that they are exempt from others, this might in certain cases amount to specifying their status *vis-à-vis* the code, but not their independence from it. To say the King is above the law is to make him subject to the law if this remark is part of the legal system. Albeit subject in a very special way, for he has only freedoms and no duties with respect to the law. If one is not subject to a certain code, its regulations are irrelevant and can make no difference to him, thus they cannot even say that he is free. It is not only the case that in terms of this code he cannot have duties, but also that he cannot have rights and/or freedoms.

It might be just as well observed here that where the basic, and most general rules of the community are concerned, their scope of application (to individuals) is simply determined by the fact that those and not other persons recognize it. But this will not serve as a solution where the rule or code applies only to a section of those who recognize the system of communal rules. If status differences are specified independently – the rule or code can refer to the individual *via* his status, thus status formation rules can form the foundation that is needed. The basic status formation rules can be of course quite general, i.e. depend for their effective scope on recognition by the respective individuals alone. Given this the emergence of rules and codes selectively relevant to some individuals rather than others can be understood. A rule can refer to its subject(s) not only by status name, but also by name – thus it could state that "Tom, Dick and Harry are to wash up every evening." This rule clearly does not name Tom, Dick and Harry, it only uses their names, and thus it relies on an earlier naming procedure to achieve the desired effect.

In objection, it would seem possible to cite at least one type of case to contradict the above tenet. A code might appear to specify when it ceases to apply. E.g. "*Officers on attaining flag rank cease to be bound by uniform regulations.*"

Two interpretations are possible of this regulation:

a) The regulation concerns dress and is a member of the code in question.

b) We have there a meta-maxim determining the scope of other regulations in the code.

If (a) is adopted as the correct interpretation the case collapses back into the one discussed above, and flag officers, like the King, are subject to the respective set of arrangements. If on the other hand (b) is adopted, the rule stands outside the code in question and poses no problem. Thus the counterexample does not work. However this is an over-simplification for it treats the respective regulations as necessarily belonging to clearly distinct and well delineated codes. This might be so in the case of codified laws, but the rules of custom, etc., could be thought of as forming an "open" system, which could in principle include any regulation that can be formulated.[12] In this case the meta-regulation could not be regarded as outside the code in question and the counterexample remains standing.

This will not do, for in the case of an open system there would be no determinable separate codes in the required sense. Is it then the case that the present point cannot be raised in such conditions? This is going too far, but the issue has to be related to fit the set-up. Instead of codes and meta-codes, it is now necessary to consider object or first order, and meta- or second order, regulations. The principle would then consist in saying that with respect to any given type of activity no respective object regulation is capable of determining the competence or the scope of itself or another object regulation, this has to be done by a meta-regulation. If it be held that this amounts to no more than defining object and meta-regulations, this interpretation is acceptable and sufficient. A code will as a rule contain both first and second order regulations. Thus the meta-regulations belonging to the code will *inter alia* limit internally the scope of some object-regulations. For clarity's sake it should be mentioned that a regulation can be meta with respect to another regulation, with respect to a code, or a system, etc.

An open system creates important possibilities of variation, but in this study codified arrangements will remain the object of discussion, mainly for reasons of simplicity and economy. With the above proviso it can be agreed: that the scope of a given particular regulation cannot be determined by the regulation itself; that the scope of a regulation within a code is often determined within this code; and that the scope of a code cannot be determined by itself. Further, it is possible that the

[12] See A. Tarski, "The Concept of Truth in Formalised Languages," in *Logic, Semantics, Metamathematics*, p. 164–5, for a relevant account of a "semantically open language" (LSM Oxford, 1956).

scope of one code be determined by another. Since meta-remarks and rules are possible about codes as well, if the code whose scope is to be determined is an object code and the determination has to be made on the meta-level then a scope of a given regulation or code can be determined by either a meta-code or a meta-regulation with respect to the given object regulation or code. Independently of this there can exist a special arrangement that determines solely *how* the scope is to be decided. For instance, the power to determine to whom this code or regulation applies can be vested in a certain authority, and this authority then can determine it by declaration.

It might be also objected that there does not seem to be anything strange in "*A*" expecting "*B*" to wash *B*'s ears every morning, and then the expectation includes the scope of the application in itself. But this is exactly what cannot happen if the above is right. The following distinctions will clarify the issue:

(a) *A regulation* is based on a *standing arrangement displaying two kinds of generality* – it applies to every case of *x* and it applies to everybody, that is, every member of the community, "as of the group in question" – such regulation cannot determine its scope for it presupposes the group – it is formulated with respect to the members of this group as such.
(b) *An order or agreement* might be *standing but is not general*. That is, it is directed at a selected number from among the people to whom the standing arrangements, in virtue of which the order or agreement is possible, could apply.
(c) *A command* is *neither standing nor general* in that it is not only directed at a selected person or persons as above, but it also specifies the precise occasion at which a certain performance is required.[13]

Clearly, commands cannot *as such* result in standing arrangements – thus a command cannot make me a member of a group to whom a certain set of rules applies, but an order or an agreement can. But then this order is not a rule belonging to the code to which I became subject as the result of it. This does not contradict the analysis offered above.[14]

The case cited above does not contradict the analysis either for it

[13] Please note that here I have sharpened the distinction between "command", "order" and "arrangement."

[14] It should be noted that the sense of "command" as developed here could not be utilised to state Austin's theory of law as a command for a *general* command is a misnomer in the present terminology. Cf. J. Austin, *The Province of Jurisprudence Determined* (1832), ed. H. L. A. Hart, Weidenfeld and Nicholson, London, 1954.

is an example of an order or agreement rather than an example of a regulation.

The above argument can again be questioned, for with respect to an open system no clear distinction between an object-system and a meta-system can be drawn. At the same time meta-remarks can be made about any rule-orientated situation possible within the system. How then can a system of arrangements be stratified, and how are we to bar membership-determining remarks from the scope of a code in question? An open system does not permit specific remarks about its limits as a whole – it can embrace any development – this potential is its defining quality.[15]

It has to be stressed that even if it belongs to an open system, a code cannot be open since it has to have limits, for it must have a definite area of authority.[16] This is so even if it is, as often can be, the case that the limits are only vaguely established *viz.* there is a wide area where *ad hoc* decision making is *necessary*. However this kind of open texture while making the system less precise in some ways does not make it open. Speaking loosely, a code, its meta-code, and the possibly open system to which they belong, can be regarded as the one unit which in a sense they are. As long as we do not regard this set unthinkingly as open in all its respects, it is easy to avoid misunderstanding. Codes cannot be open even when they are vague. Nor are they open simply because they belong to an open system. Consequently no conclusions, about codes and/or rules, which are in a similar position, can be drawn from the fact that the respective system is open. Codes and rules still are formal and must meet formal requirements, *inter alia* they cannot have consequences on individuals and matters beyond their scope. If the community is an open system then if its membership is determined by actual recognition[17] the openness of the system creates no difficulty, for actual recognition is a fact and not a rule of any kind.

To sum up – the scope of a code can be established by a meta-code, a meta-regulation or a meta-maxim. If this was the only way an infinite regress would be unavoidable. Direct recognition alone seems to offer a solution to this dilemma.

People who are bound by communal regulations form a community, and these regulations form the bond between them. Individuals are members of the same community if and only if they are generally pre-

[15] Cf. A. Tarski, *Logic, Semantics and Metamathematics*, Oxford, 1956, p. 164–5, for a relevant discussion of a natural language.

[16] *Vide* Chapter I, p. 25 ff.

[17] *Vide* p. 132.

pared to seriously regard their mutual expectations as positive reasons for acting. Now this *need not be determined either formally or explicitly*. Inasmuch as X is prepared to regard and regards some of the expectations of John Doe, Richard Roe and other members of the group as reasons for his actions, and inasmuch as they are prepared and do take some of X's expectations seriously, they are members of the same community. This of course is only one aspect of the story. *Now* it may be simply an empirical fact depending on there being such mutual recognition, that someone belongs to one community and not to another, and a matter of empirical investigation what are the limits of this, that or another community. Further complications come about because *communal expectations* representing the attitude of most of the members of the community do arise. All this is *only possible* if the initial condition of mutual respect and recognition is satisfied. In sophisticated circumstances people who sufficiently lack such respect, and who earn similar disrespect *by* others are said to be antisocial.

Clearly if the membership of a community is regarded as an empirical fact, the question of the determination of the scope of, at least, the most general of the rules, need not arise. In such cases all such ground rules can be regarded as *applying to everybody*, that is, to everybody who might find himself in the contingent situation in which the particular rule is relevant. Whom the members of the group regard as a possible value for "everybody" is an empirical matter decided by recognition. From the point of view of an outsider such a person is simply a member of this particular group. But then an outsider could describe this collection of individuals as a community. The fact that there are other similar groups does not make it necessary for those who abide by the rules forming one of them to think of these rules as applying to members of a specific group of people as such. It is possible for the members of this group to treat other people like they treat animals or birds – and never even consider them as possible objects of respect, recognition and/or subjects of rules. In such a case anybody who would be thought of as a possible subject of rules, that is, come within the circle of mutual respect and recognition, would become a member of the overall community automatically; for he would be included in the concept of "everybody" – to whom any communal rule could in an appropriate case apply. If the rule does not apply he simply has a freedom (or sometimes a liberty), but in principle as somebody he is subject to this and other rules in all of these cases – he is within their scope – everybody is. If it is replied that e.g. members of another tribe are outside the rules – the reply is that they are not somebodies. Similarly we do not think of animals or inanimate objects as possible members of human groups and this quite clearly need not involve us in writing the difference between a human being and an inanimate material object, or say a cat, into the system in which our rules are expressed. Similarly there is a difference between saying that the fact that people forming a community must in fact be a separate group of people among people, and saying that this must be formally taken note of in a social system which they could operate.

The last will explain how the scope of arrangements can be determined in primitive and in ultimate cases. In less primitive cases, and in cases of groups within the community, the scope of arrangements usually will be determined by orders or agreements. However, it should be remembered that while orders must be explicit, agreements could be tacit and unformulated.

The scope of a regulation within a code can be determined by a meta-rule stating to whom the regulation is to apply: only to ladies; only to typhoid carriers; only to members of parliament; etc.

To determine status differences between people, for example between ladies and gentlemen, amounts to dividing the group into sub-classes. A sub-class as used here is not in any way separately organised. It is merely a *discernible section of the population* which may, but need not, be significant. The division can go in any number of ways: by the colour of hair; sex; age; height; weight; *x*'ing;[18] etc.. Special rights, freedoms or duties can be given to any sub-class, provided that it can be discerned as a class, even a class by enumeration, thus it is a basis for complexity. The socially significant differentation is determined by the rule of the group, for discernible sub-classes can be treated completely equally, e.g. those who do, *vs* those who do not, eat breakfast. The social inequalities that exist are created almost entirely by rules, and their differential treatment with respect to discernible individuals or sub-classes of the population.

The problem of status differences applying to people who do not form natural sub-classes may now be considered again. For instance, blondes are a natural sub-class, judges are not. In the case of judges, or officers of the Army, it seems that the rules themselves have created the sub-classes in question. In this there lies a problem. For the sub-class exists only because its members were given the particular status they have. As seen above declaring someone to be an officer, or consecrating

[18] *Vide* p. 61 above.

someone as a priest, will not provide sufficient explanation how individuals acquire status, for those words would be meaningless unless they specify the status this person is to have, and this presupposes that the respective position already exists. How then is status to be specified unless it can be determined *who* has the special duties, rights and freedoms?

It could be decided quite independently and *a prima vista* that *whoever* has the right to declare the proceedings of the court open *also* has the right to declare them closed, and *as well* the right to adjourn the proceedings for any time he thinks fit, etc. This specification creates a cluster of special duties and similarly a cluster of freedoms or of liberties can be created. A single cluster could include all three. This then could be called a *status formula*. In terms of a status formula a position can be determined. A formula for a judge, a formula for a defendant, etc. etc. are possible. The problem then lies in specifying how people are to be fitted to the different formulae. It was suggested above, that this could be done by *X*'ing,[19] but how does this work in possible practice? Many ways are of course possible, e.g.: *whoever* is caught by the police in an apparent breach of the law can in a certain approved form be placed in the position of a defendant; *whoever* is appointed by the proper authority is to assume the position of judge; similarly, elections are held in order to determine who will be: the leader of the Opposition; the leader of the Government; etc. etc. Artificial or conventional sub-classes of people can thus be established, the difference between their respective members and others being defined in terms of how certain rules apply to them, the membership determined by procedures instituted with the help of other rules. All this is only possible where positions can be determined relatively independently of determining the personal status of an actual member of the community.

This is a sophisticated procedure which could not be duplicated by mere mutual recognition, but it would seem *possible* for a non-natural sub-class to arise indirectly in a simpler manner. Suppose now that whenever a group of people belonging to the given community are detached from it they select a leader, and that once someone is selected he tends, and it becomes his prerogative, to again assume leadership in similar circumstances. This will create a non-natural sub-class of group leaders, differentiated from others not only by their history but by their present general status, but not distinguished by any natural difference from them.

[19] *Vide* p. 62.

In a case of a non-natural status-bearing sub-class, this sub-class is determined by rules usually including formation rules and *X*'ing rules. These rules apply to those who fulfil certain conditions, and these conditions need not include natural differences. This explains the existence of status differences operating independently of natural differences, but does not exclude the existence of natural difference-bound status. Status can be ascribed to any class of individuals in a community, provided only that its membership can be determined, and that only members of the community are involved. (Thus a relevant subclass would be for example American Negroes, not negroes in general.)

For clarity's sake it should be added here that it is impossible to create only one status, though it is possible to create only one status difference. The formation rules must specify inequalities between two subclasses α and β – if *alphas* receive in these terms a privileged status of a certain kind, the *betas* will *mutatis mutandis* receive a complementary non-privileged status. This is so obvious that once mentioned it need not be argued.

It is also an obvious fact that the membership of the sub-class must be narrower than the membership of the community, for otherwise it would be impossible to treat people differentially. Any sub-class, whether it has special status or not, might begin to be organized like a group in its own right. That is, it may acquire not only status, but also a structure of its own. This, however, is the subject of the next chapter, here it will suffice to remark that once it begins to acquire special organization it acquires *ipso facto* a corresponding status position. Clearly when this happens the large group becomes divided into those who do, and those who do not belong to the sub-group in question. There will be a set of rules applying to the first class of individuals only.

CHAPTER IV

SUB-COMMUNITIES AND SUB-STRUCTURES

The type of community permitted by the elements discussed in previous chapters is in some sense one-dimensional. The concepts allow a fairly involved group structure but the complexity lies in the subtlety and differentiation of the internal organization of the one group which displays the structure. *Thus sub-classes are possible but not sub-structures*. Yet communities as we know them contain also sub-structures, i.e. bodies of people forming what might be called branch communities, organizations, etc. These have *some structure in their own right,* and are a significant development in the complexity of the ultimate body.

A sub-structure, unlike a sub-class, has some of the character of a community. In some respects it is capable of action as a unit, and its members are capable of acting in concert in much the same fashion in which members of a community are. There are many examples: policemen act as members of the police force and the entire organization presents some sort of unified face; a member of a big business organization often acts as a member of this organization and the whole organization behaves in some unified manner. The difference between a substructure and a community lies roughly in this – that a community is more comprehensive and more independent, it has a wider scope, but both are organized, and the organization of both is to be understood in terms of the concepts analysed above, *viz.* regulation, status, etc.

It could be objected plausibly that to say that a community is more comprehensive than a sub-structure is insufficient, for both communities and organizations which merit the name of a sub-structure allow differing degrees of comprehensiveness. For instance, a small rural community is much less comprehensive than Imperial Chemical Industries Limited. It encompasses fewer people, the people are concentrated in a much smaller area than those connected with I.C.I.; finally it might be claimed that I.C.I. exerts a much tighter control on its members than does a small rural community, that it makes a much greater impression on their lives and that it is involved in more varied dealings. But I.C.I. still requires a community (or communities) in order to exist, unless it were to change its character quite radically.

This is all true but it is concerned with the wrong sort of encompassing or inclusiveness. Organizations such as Imperial Chemical Industries do not only transcend small rural communities, they transcend states as there are branches of this particular firm in England, Australia, the countries of the Common Market, New Zealand, the United States and many others. But no one would say, on this ground, that I.C.I. is a more comprehensive structure than the Commonwealth of Australia, or Great Britain, so what kind of inclusiveness is required of a community?

Again it could be claimed that such an organization e.g. I.C.I. could affect the lives of its members more than do some of the communities (e.g. parishes, towns, etc.) to which they belong. This sounds plausible particularly when we think in terms of the felt influences – a man might have to think of I.C.I. more often than of the town-community. But this view is far too narrow – a structure such as I.C.I. takes a group of people *already subject to communal rules*, and organizes them *further*, often in a very far-reaching way. But very significantly they need not be so organized, they can live in the community before I.C.I. comes, and after it leaves. If the town is a community it cannot be removed without replacement. Unlike I.C.I. it has an essential role to perform, if it goes it has to be replaced, for it is impossible to have communal life without belonging to a community. All this allows considerable further complexity that will to at least some extent be discussed later.[1]

For the present moment we shall in reply just stress the point that community is more comprehensive than a communal sub-structure not in terms of the number of people involved, the size of the area they inhabit, the conscious impression it creates, etc., but in proportion to how many areas of their life are involved in the organization, how many essential arrangements and inter-personal arrangements are provided by this body of rules, etc. I.C.I. is narrow in those terms; it *primarily* concerns only business activity and employees earning power. Since one might, and far too often does, suit even moral views to one's business interests, other areas might be indirectly affected. But this effect is secondary while the employee's duties in the office or shop are

[1] In fact all this obtains when we have a first order sub-community – this type of complexity is discussed *infra*.

not. Further, a number of activities cannot be determined by internal rules of organizations such as I.C.I. from the point of view of, for example, legal propriety. They are the concern of the law of the country. Health regulations, traffic codes, criminal law, social customs and many others came to mind as examples. There is of course nothing to prevent a company, e.g. Mitsubishi, from moving into those areas of control, but if it does, it will at some stage become a community rather than just a business organization.

A group can be regarded as a community when the life of its members is orientated towards, and its style determined by, the rules and regulations that form its structure, provided always that it has sufficient scope, and becomes the main such overall influence, with respect to the *majority* of its members. Marginally it is possible for some individuals to hover between two or more communities, especially when there is no definite clash of interests and loyalties between them.[2] The impression that no one can belong to more than one community at the same time for only one can be *the main overall influence* on his life is incorrect. Quite clearly there need not exist the one and only main influence on one's life for more than one can be roughly on par with each other. If such influences are exerted by alternative communities we have the choice between saying that the individual in question belongs equally to both (or all) of these communities, or saying that he belongs to no community at all – the second is obviously implausible for his life is community orientated in any case.[3]

However there is a limit to this. Let us think of a situation where John Doe lives within two communities A and B. When relations between them are good no difficulties need arise. But let us say that the relations worsen and that it becomes a criminal offence in A to be a Jehovah's Witness, while it becomes a criminal offence in B to fail to be a Jehovah's Witness. Suppose further that both rules concern the behaviour of the citizens of A and B in and out of their community. Clearly John Doe cannot comply with the rules of both communities – he has to choose between them. Where two communities are independent of each other such a conflict can always arise; it if does double loyalty becomes impossible and the dictates of one only of the different groups can be internalised. It is of course possible to have what might be termed a guest-status – thus an ambassador from

[2] The relations here hinted at can become very complex and puzzling where there are both sub-communities and sub-structures in which the individuals are involved.

[3] Difficulties can arise with respect to a possible "citizen of the world" who is a guest in any particular community, but those are not difficulties in principle.

a Communist country is safe in a state where Communism is outlawed – yet a guest is not a member of the community in question, for a community cannot consist of guests alone. Moreover, if John Doe declares himself a guest in *B* and citizen of *A* he is not a citizen of both at once. Thus if one were to be a citizen of more than one independent community at the same time his status as such will always be qualified.

We can then say that a given individual is a member of a given community if he is ultimately bound by this community's rules and regulations rather than being bound by the rules and regulations of any other group of people. An individual is a member of a communal substructure if he is bound by the rules and regulations of this structure in the area where it is competent but *in other areas*, and *whenever there is a clash* he is bound by the rules and regulations of a specifiable community. Both the elements are important, for if the area of competence of a body is not limited it is in no way different from a sub-community; at the same time if the rules of the parent community do not take precedence over the rules of the member sub-structure or sub-community, then the putative sub-unit is not part of the ultimate body but an alien intrusion.[4] Such might have been colonialist trading posts in foreign lands – supported in their impudent independence by the colonising governments of the powers that sponsored them.

This kind of test will not provide a hard and fast line between what is a community and what a sub-structure. It leaves many matters the province of judgement. Clearly a sub-community is a community, that is the rules of this unit must be sufficient to determine the style of life of its members, short of this the unit could still be a sub-structure provided only that it is sufficiently organized as a body. In practice it might be very difficult to decide which is the case.

To illustrate take a small industrial area possessed of a very strong trade union organization, such as the Barrier Reef Industrial Council. Assume that the Council determines: jobs, pay, hotel hours, the value of public works, education and to a large extent censorship, land sales, house and other loans, acceptability for permanent residence, etc. but does not control: taxes, courts, foreign passports, etc. Is the union organization a community or simple a communal sub-structure. Now reasons can be given for both views, the decision might be difficult to reach, but it is easier to argue about the involvement of its members in

[4] Clearly a community *a* is the sub-unit of community *A* if and only if the precedence rules concern all or most of the members of *a vis-à-vis A*.

the trade union organization, about the range and scope of union rules, etc., than in unspecific terms about the "communityhood" of the organization itself.

A community may consist of a number of smaller communities. If this is the case, we might say in a very good sense that those smaller communities are its sub-structures and thus we have another kind of complexity not discussed before. So, for instance, the City of London is a community; the state of Victoria in the Commonwealth of Australia is a community, and yet, at the same time, they are parts of such bigger communities as the Commonwealth of Australia, the United Kingdom, etc. There can be more than two steps in this process, for Victoria can consist in a number of smaller communities, and they can break up into smaller units still. Only the size of the country, the number of people living in it and their national and private character will determine where this development will stop.

Two types of distinction are then necessary: one (a) between *sub-structures* which are not communities and *communities*, illustrated by the difference between the State of Victoria on one hand and Imperial Chemical Industries on the other. And the other (b) between the *ultimate community* and the *sub-communities* that go into the making of it. This exemplified by the United States on one hand, and the State of New York on the other.

Let us take the second distinction (b) first. The community formed by the people living in Bairnsdale is of a lesser order than the State of Victoria. Wherein lies the difference? In this case, the large overall community tends to be political, a sub-community non-political. In the small community the ties between its members tend to be both immediate and natural. A significant proportion of the actions of a member of this community is reasonably directly relevant to the type of life anyone can have in the community in question, e.g. Bairnsdale. Fewer actions of a Victorian are relevant to the style of life of every other Victorian, and they tend to be so in a more remote fashion. There seems to be no reason to suppose that an action of a Mildura taxi driver in its own right need have any reasonably direct effect on the life of a bank manager in Melbourne. Sometimes it will be only because certain general policies and aims are embodied in the organization of the entire community, together with the fact that the way in which they are pursued, and the measure of success with which they are implemented, affects the life of every citizen that there exists a common bond between given members of this large group. The bond exists because in the end it is such actions that determine the communal style of life. Even on a general level it is possible to act either in accord with the general standards of the community or out of step with them; in the first case the existing set-up is strengthened, in the second weakened, and if a sufficient number of habitual violations do occur it itself will tend to change, for arrangements alter to suit what is usually done, though not always as explicitly as with the 85% speed limit system.[5] The fact that a single action can have every little effect on its own only illustrates the stability and ponderousness of communal structure – which increases with the size of the unit.

It should be noted that where communities of different levels are concerned, the higher order community might, at least to some extent, fail to prescribe directly, in a considerable number of areas of possible communal behaviour – instead of this a limit would be placed on what direct rules are admissible in member communities – thus different states in Australia have different traffic codes, but it is not open to one of them (or this could be so) to introduce unilaterally the right hand traffic rule, nor are they free to introduce either multiple or homosexual marriages. While there is perhaps no commanding reason for these restrictions, other possible differences could be much more disruptive.

It is not easy to draw a line between public and private actions, but it can be accepted at least provisionally that an action is public in a wide sense (a) if some actual communal rules are in fact relevant to it or (b) if it might have effects that come under such rules, or (c) most weakly of all, such communal rules might, should or are likely to be established to deal with this kind of action. An action might be public in either of the three ways cited above and yet be regarded as private on some other grounds. For instance it can be held that it is not proper or advisable to have rules interfering with this or that type of case.

Actions can be regarded as public in a narrower sense if they are public on the first test (a), and are not held to be private on any other. They could be held to be public in the strict sense if they cannot be held to be private on any ground, but it is dubious whether any actions come into this category.[6]

A large overall community is in one good sense of the word *political*,

[5] In this system the speed limit is revised periodically so as to be maintained at a figure representing the average speed of 85% of the motorists using the highway.

[6] Completely private experiences, desires, motives, etc. are completely outside the province of rules, but then they are not actions either.

because in this type of community there is no need for direct relevance of any action of one person to the action of another, and the most important relevance is constituted by the effect on all people of the general *policies and aims* of the society. The effects of those *aims and policies* of a society on its members might be *sufficient* in some cases to form a community of some order. This sort of relation can be regarded as typical for a *political community.* For a sub-political community a direct relevance of the actions of people to the lives of other members of this community is typical.

It is of course possible for hierarchical relations to exist between political and non-political groups. In consequence, what might be termed structural considerations are needed to determine the relative positions of supra and sub-communities. However, there is considerable plausibility in the tenet that supra-community will tend to be more, sub-community less, political. In a political body typical communal expectations will relate to matters of general policy. This creates a problem, for if there exists a set of expectations which centre on matters of policy, *viz.* common defence, tariff, foreign policy, etc., their arrangements centred on those general and not immediate matters probably would not be sufficient to form a community. A group structure comprising general policy rules *alone* cannot work for it cannot offer sufficient directions concerning particular actions. A purely political community might appear thus to be like a top storey of a building without foundations and ground floor. In practice, no community needs to be purely or predominantly political, and it not only can but would tend to comprise direct relevance rules together with others. Sometimes the rules of direct relevance will be relegated to the smaller units which comprise the overall community, and it is these sub-units that tend to be communities in their own right. They will usually comprise most of the direct relevance rules that are needed to make the system work. The distribution of arrangements can be stratified, thus typically the state will control more *immediate* matters than the Commonwealth; the local government more *direct* than the state government, etc.

Both ways of dealing with immediate matters coexist often in one and the same community. Thus there can exist sub-communities that regulate matters such as milk delivery, building regulations, etc., and at the same time there can exist rules and institutions belonging to the structure of the ultimate political community that deal with immediate matters of similar kind; for example, the postal service, the health services, etc.

But the picture is still oversimplified. All the sub-communities belonging to a larger structure could share a number of rules of behaviour that are essentially controlled on their level; in fact they most often do. But it is not necessary that this or that particular rule should be shared. Thus in one place there might be strict rules concerning noise, in others none. The best example of relative differentiations might be provided by medieval cities – they enjoyed a style of life quite different from that of other comparable sub-communities in their states.

The question is: when the rules are shared by all, i.e. they range over sub-communities, do they just happen to be similar, or do they constitute elements of the structure of the larger communal body?

One is tempted to say that they merely happen to be similar if the existence of this similarity is not binding on the sub-communities in question and if the expectation of similarity is not accepted as a reason for it.[7] Clearly there is a number of possible stages between the complete acceptance of such an expectation of uniformity and its complete rejection. It is also quite possible that a certain level of similarity is expected but not uniformity on any given point.

Clearly, even if it was the case that the supra-community failed to supply all or most of the basic direct relevance rules necessary, ground level arrangements on the level of sub-communities would still have to be shared to a large extent by all sub-groups, in a given overall higher order community. The reason for this lies in the fact that the existence of very wide differences in some respects would make the system unworkable. To illustrate say that in Gretna Green it is possible to get a quick divorce and this is unique. A situation easily imaginable. But imagine that England, Wales and Scotland did not recognize each other's marriages at all – this would clearly lead to chaos, and put some strain on the communal unity of Great Britain. Too many of such strains could test it severely. It might be usefully noted that this fact might make it more difficult to decide whether a given rule common to many sub-communities is part of the super-structure, or consists in no more than agreement between sub-structures.

However big and sophisticated the ultimate structure, it must be based on a large number of shared communal direct relevance expectations, even though the manner in which they are in fact generally accepted is not prescribed, the only condition being effectiveness.[8] Thus

[7] I.e. if there is no overall policy on the matter.

[8] One can think of sub-unit based arrangements that conform on supra-level for policy reasons as the epitome of federalism.

it need not be important in practice to be able to answer the question posed at the end of the above paragraph. A sub-community is one not only in virtue of what distinguishes it from other groups in the large structure. For it is a member of the larger body in that it shares a number of basic expectations with other relevant groups. Consequently it can, and almost invariably will, have its own rules based on expectations identical with those on which rules of another sub-community are based. The question of the range of a communal expectation is a vexing one.

How are we to decide in a supra-community A comprising sub-communities a_1, a_2, a_3, a_4, etc., that the alleged ground rules r_1, r_2, r_3, r_4, etc. belonging to the respective sub-communities and identical in form are in fact separate rather than being a parent community-rule R as applied in these units?

The obvious test is who administers and sustains them – for a rule can be directly based on supra-expectations, e.g. "Let us defend every inch of our national territory" or sub-expectation, e.g. "Let people in our neighbourhood observe silence after 11 p.m.". The first is a national the second a local rule. A problem arises for it is possible to have a state law on noise after 11 p.m. and there could be a supra-expectation that all sub-communities shall conform to a certain standard for instance regarding the rule of law. In the first case the state law could enforce in a community a_x a rule that is not in fact consonant with the wishes of the members of a_x – this could happen with gambling laws unpopular in frontier communities, who could prefer also to settle their disputes by personal combat rather than in a court of Law, thus going against a supra-expectation.

A simple test whether a_x administers these rules would be in determining whether it can follow its own recalcitrant wishes. But matters are not simple, for the cost of doing this might be considered too high,[9] and members of a_x might have a loyalty to A with their regional feelings, so they do they might conform. If they need not be regarded as conforming to a supra-rule, they might be conforming to a supra-policy or maxim, and implementing ground level sub-community rules in accordance with it.

This is clearly the case where the gambling restrictions and rules of law requirement are contained in a_x's by-laws policed by a_x's officers, but issues are not always that clear-cut.

It could be observed that it is in fact possible for a community to

[9] E.g. tax concessions might be lost.

conform to an outside maxim, even if this maxim is not a maxim of its parent-community. Thus a contraception-desiring population, all of them Roman Catholics, could make laws against contraception in conformity with the known policy of their church. Consequently the fact that this kind of relationship exists is not in itself a proof that the policy-determining body is a supra-community with respect to the directed group. In practice conflicts can arise between policies demanded by the state and outside bodies, nor are they confined to the behaviour of sub-communities.

Lastly we might say that if it were the case with respect to any rule R/r_x that if a sub-community a_x were to choose to substitute for it $\sim r_x$ then it would be considered as breaking away from the parent community A, it would follow that R/r_x is a parent community rule.

Accepting an oversimplification it could be said that sub-communities belonging to the same overall community share the same ultimate set of rules. Even if these can be variously implemented in different sub-communities. This is not true of say a business empire and a football club, even if both exist in the same community, for their rule basis is too narrow to give rise to communal organization, and as far as the community is concerned all the members of such an organization are directly subject to communal rules. The rules of the club for instance are then quite separate and their status is determined by the fact that the individuals are permitted by their community to band together and make such rules within certain limits. The necessary similarity between the rules of such organizations are determined then by these limits. Thus the law can state that rules of corporate bodies are not enforceable on its members unless they are made in a given form, certain agreements might be forbidden, etc. etc. Here again in complex actual situations the distinctions might not be easy to apply, but it would be surprising if it were.

In general we can say that sub-communities *form a larger community* – organizations do not, they *operate within it.* This is their defining difference, and it can be used as a criterion. The only way in which it could be empirically refuted would be by showing that the distinction cannot be used to advantage in organizing observational data.

The majority of regulations appertaining to the members of a sub-community in at least one good sense can be regarded as *their set of rules*, for these would be intelligible even if we made no reference to any other structure including the parent community.

The obvious expectation is constituted by supra-community direct relevance rules, for there the enforcement etc. systems rest without the sub-community. Even in those cases it is usually easy to envisage the contraction of these to within the sub-community in question, except where the rules are forced upon it against the will of its members, e.g. the pigtail forced on the Chinese by their Manchu conquerors. Such contraction could be viewed as severing the links with the parent-body but need not mean more than the gaining of relative independence, the workings of the unit in question could remain unaffected in almost every other respect. Thus a sub-community can be regarded as a separable unit, and it could be agreed that to the extent to which a unit is not thus separable it should be regarded as failing to be a community, though it might still be a sub-body of another kind.

A rule of thumb criterion of separability can be found in the fact that in principle a sub-community should find it possible to continue to exist as a community on its own, even if it was thereby impoverished. In contradistinction a lesser sub-structure can exist only within a community.

Members of a sub-community would as a rule be members of the larger unit *by way of being its members.*[10] This is not the case with a communal organization, even in cases where it is as a matter of fact impossible for members of the community to escape a membership of one or more organizations. To a question : "Are you an Australian?" the answer, "Of course, I come from Tasmania" is appropriate, but "Of course, I work for Repco" or "Of course, I am with the Commonwealth Immigration Department" are not. If there was a rule limiting the membership of these two bodies to Australians, one could make the point by reference to the rule, but no such move is needed in the case of a genuine sub-community.

It should be kept in mind that a *sub-structure* is not just a sub-class within the community, and that therefore it must have some structure which confers on it more than just the peculiarity of status that could be enjoyed by members of a mere sub-class. Yet to say that a substructure is not a community is to deny that it possesses certain structural characteristics. More particularly, it will not possess sufficient scope to make it basically sufficient to orient the lives of its members as a whole. Still there exists some similarity between a sub-structure and a community. An organization must be capable of acting as a

[10] One cannot live in England but not in any part of it, but to live in a part of it is to live within a sub-community. An exception is an Englishman living permanently abroad, for he is a Briton, and the only status he has in a ground level community, e.g. Iceland, is that of a guest.

unit, its members able to act in unison. To enter an organization is to accept the rules governing this body. If one is a member of a commercial organization, one *ipso facto* accepts the rules of this organization. Within such organization, like in a community, there exists a body of expectations shared in a familiar fashion by its members. Members of a club may agree that no one should be admitted to the club if he is black-balled by any member; that no one is to bring in women. They might agree to *share and/or proselytize certain beliefs, etc. etc.* Every organization will have to have this *rule gestalt* which will determine the behaviour of members insofar as it is relevant to their being members, even if its scope is essentially narrower than is the case with the *rule gestalt* of a community.

The difference between an organization and a community lies in that a sub-structure will typically concern a well-defined and relatively narrow area of behaviour. Thus a club is concerned with the spending of leisure hours by its members when at the club. A church is concerned with the religious behaviour of its members. A commercial enterprise is concerned with the job of its members and what they do to earn their money. But there is no such well-defined area in the case of a community as such, here anything that someone does might be a matter of interest and control. A community though restricted in membership is an open organization where kinds of activities are concerned, anything that could be subject to rules can be its province; a sub-structure is a closed organization on both counts.

The sub-structure (non-community) can be perhaps characterized by what can be, and is generally left out of its rule structure. It may be concerned with any area of behaviour, but then any area, or areas, can be left out. So it need not provide for law and order; for safety; for *modus vivendi* between people of violently, if permissibly, different persuasions; for arbitration in case of important disputes, etc. Thus if what can be seen to be an essential area(s) of inter-personal relations is (are) left out of a rule structure of a certain group, it is not a (sub) community. It might be safely said that if there are no such omissions it would be misleading to call the group in question an organization.

Now this is not to say that a community interferes, or must interfere with everything possible, for many areas might be, should be, and in fact are, free. But the competence or the scope of communal interest is not limited within well-defined confines, and it is *not limited by the fact that it is a community.* Nothing is out of bounds as a communal matter, though it could be claimed that in this or that matter people should be free. Where an organization is concerned the competence of its directives is *limited by the stated or understood aim of the organization.* Thus since the pursuit of philosophy and the furthering of the interest in philosophy is the stated aim of the Australasian Association of Philosophy, it is not competent to rule on political matters, e.g. the propriety of Australian involvement in Vietnam, simply because the latter issue has nothing to do with philosophy.

Now in different conditions different areas of behaviour that could be controlled can be left without control even in a community and some of them might be of prime importance. It should be noted that taking the set of areas that are both important and controlled in a given set-up, all, or almost all, of them will be under the control of a given community, most of them would not be under the control of a given organization.[11] Some organizations will control none of them, e.g. the philatelist union. Thus the distinction is achieved by the criterion of scope of the competence of a community vs. an organization: the scope of communal control is in principle limited to the pursuit of a specifiable goal, though this might be quite wide (e.g. a religious order), but the basic overall foundation must come from the community in question. In practice even a sub-community can accept most of its structure from the parent community by, in a way, internalizing the relevant arrangements. The scope of their fully independent rules can thus remain quite small concerning, e.g. just their streets, beaches and gardens. But this is an entirely different matter for an organization having perhaps more independent rules than such a sub-community, *it need not internalize* the rules that are not included in its structure, it need not show any interest in them. They are communal matters, and communal rules are taken for granted in setting up an organization. The organization need not even be sympathetic towards them. It would be strange if Londoners did not feel themselves to be British, but members of I.C.I. need not, though they can. In ordinary parlance the distinction is less strict than the one envisaged here, nor is it in fact clear, or easy to apply in practice.

Sub-structures have *rules of their own,* but compliance with them is not to be expected of other members of the community *qua* members.

[11] The problem of morals is of a different order, it could be maintained that moral convictions are of the wrong kind, i.e. that moral behaviour *cannot* be controlled by any regulation, and does not lend itself to social engineering. A community is competent to control anything and everything that can be controlled. Notwithstanding this it could be held, e.g. on moral, religious or pragmatic grounds, that certain pursuits should not be controlled, that it would be either wrong or inadvisable to control them, etc.

Thus, if x does not work in B.H.P., no one expects x to arrive in the B.H.P. building at 9 a.m. for work even if all his acquaintances work for B.H.P., and he lives in a B.H.P. owned town. But people are expected to accept rules that are regarded as rules of the community, provided only that they are living within the same communal group. Thus nudists are required to seek a secluded spot for group nudity, and a person coming from a subcommunity where late parties are allowed, must accept limits imposed on them by the sub-community which is his host at the moment.

A fair amount of deviation can be tolerated in this respect, thus non-conformism is possible particularly where it does not concern central issues. Nudism is more acceptable than Murder Incorporated. Another problem is created by refusal to internalise some rules on the part of some members of the community – Moslems might resent monogamy. Here too a reasonable amount of deviation is not fatal whether it takes the form of unwilling compliance or open deviation but clearly both the types of deviation are possible only against the background of the acceptance of the majority of rules by the majority of members.

One does not cease to be a member of the community on leaving or joining an organization. If one leaves a sub-community one would, unless he accepts some substitute.[12] This does not mean that he has to join another sub-community in all cases. Where it is possible to be a direct member of the larger community-unit, one can become this, but cannot renounce all rules that bound him in the sub-community. It is impossible to renounce *all* that makes one an acceptable citizen of Victoria and remain a satisfactory citizen of Australia, for in the second case it is necessary to accept a number of rules which also bind citizens of Victoria *qua* citizens of Victoria. This raises the very complex question of the relation between a citizen and his community. In this area it is possible to think of almost endless forms of association. The rules of a communal organization are superimposed on, or presuppose the existence of, community rules; this alone makes the existence of the body possible. In a sub-community these rules are *incorporated* as rules of this very (sub) community. These points of course do not determine how larger communities have to be internally organized, but they can be used to determine which of their elements are communities and which are not.

It has to be observed that organizations and membership of organizations can be recognized in a community, and that communal arrange-

[12] Always excepting the man who lives in a foreign land.

ments and rules can be woven around such memberships, and finally that this can be incorporated in communal structure just as much as personal qualities can. If a community can be organized to suit the personality of a Man, say Hitler, Xerxes or Napoleon, it can be organized to suit an organization or organizations, say the Church in mediaeval times, or business firms in a thoroughly capitalist set-up. A good example is provided by the Stock Exchange in some countries, e.g. Australia. But this does not have to be done, and such commitments are not of the essence of communal life. It is the feature of a community that it is capable of incorporating into its structure anything about which public arrangements and rules *can be made.* This is plenty but not all, for instance the areas of private morality, personal taste, individual interests, etc. do not lend themselves to social engineering and cannot be organized in this fashion, because they cannot be effectively controlled by rules.

There are of course similarities between organizations and sub-communities. Both a branch community and an organization are limited by the community to which they belong. That is, they can have their own special and particular rules, but those cannot go counter to the rules of the community within which the organization in question is contained, otherwise the whole would be at loggerheads with itself. This kind of tension might possibly exist in exceptional cases, but the extent to which such contradictions can be contained in a structure is limited for beyond a certain point it would force the community to disintegrate for obvious reasons.

Each *sub-structure* is based on a set of rules. This set must be a code, for members of an organization will have banded together because of a project or a special interest, and those rules will determine how they should behave in a number of contingencies connected with their special pursuit.[13] A code is a cluster of regulations having competence over a well-defined area of activity such as can be the province of an organization. Some codes, for example, the code of manners, would apply to every member of the community as such, some apply only to members of a given body. An organization concerns a separate group of people, usually members of one community, who are united in engaging in a certain pursuit or pursuits. Such a group sometimes can transgress communal and even national boundaries; what makes them into members of one organization is that they are selected, dedicated and organized to follow this or that specific pursuit or pursuits together. Despite this the

[13] *Vide* Chapter I, p. 24 ff.

members of this organization are subject to the respective communal rules *vis-à-vis* each of the communities in which they operate – thus their citizenship has not the inter-community character the organization has. What is more this organization in any community (state) belongs to this community (state). Even if there is one governing body, it must comply with the respective rules of each community separately.

Usually a sub-structure is narrower in membership than its parent community and can then be called an organization, or an institution, *within* this group. However it is possible for an organization to involve every citizen, this was for instance the aim of the Church in mediaeval times. Even if this is achieved it is not clear that the rules of this organization become directly communal. Let us suppose that there is a communal rule making Church membership compulsory and that this is a strictly national Church. Still the compulsory membership rule will exclude foreign emissaries, who would not normally be permitted to commit murder or drive on the wrong side of the road. The introduction of complete diplomatic immunity does not really change this situation, for a non-believer emissary will not be regarded as a criminal inaccessible to the law. For instance his deviant religious beliefs will not lead to a request that he should be recalled home, but the breach of an ordinary law will. Thus it is possible to distinguish communal from organizational rules even in such a case, for the diplomat will have to take part in communal but not in Church life, albeit the distinction exhibits all the features of open texture.

It is almost impossible for the code on which an organization is based to have the desired organizational effect unless the rules specify status differences between its members. These rules will enjoin, permit or guarantee something to the members *qua* members. So in this capacity people will have duties, freedoms and rights. A director of an organization has the right to tell people in the organization what to do, has to see to it that the organization achieves its aims, has certain freedoms, etc. Other members will have different duties, freedoms and rights, but all those rights, privileges and duties, operate from within the institution and apply to actions concerned with this particular institution as such, and not otherwise. Thus a salesman might have the right to a certain bonus payment if he sells above a certain quantity of goods, but he only has this right in his capacity as a salesman belonging to a certain commercial organization, and no other. It is a significant change when an entitlement to superannuation ceases to be an internal arrangement of this or that organization and becomes a communal, or state matter.

A viable organization not involving any internal status difference could in principle arise on a very primitive level but in practice almost all communal bodies will display enough sophistication to involve standing positions.

Ad hoc teams of relatively short duration, and not only standing communal organizations, are possible. Since these have no real permanence the status differences involved cannot be standing from the point of view of the community for they cannot be more stable than the team. The statuses if any will then be standing relatively to the team.[14] Thus there would be, for instance, the position of a captain of the team as long as the team exists. This does not exclude the possibility of an *ad hoc* rôle being accepted by someone, for example, take the rule that for as long as a player happens to be nearest to his own goalpost, he is the goalie.

It is thus possible to discern: *communal status*, held with respect to the community as such, *organization status*, held within a body, and short-term *team status*. All status positions would be either one or the other of these, provided only that status can be held also with respect to a sub-community. The difference between *status proper* and an *ad hoc* rôle should be borne in mind at this point, for an *ad hoc* rôle could be imposed also on communal or an organizational basis, and thus the distinctions superimposed on one another can produce a fairly complex classification of the possible standing of an individual *vis-à-vis* his group.

The different possibilities listed above can be utilised to produce complex forms of social intercourse. To take a relatively simple example: unless the positions of a judge, the plaintiff, counsel, and many others are defined, there could not be a sitting of a court, and no procedure resembling the one which is actually followed could be established. Let us assume that the position of the *presiding judge ad hoc* re a given court sitting can only be occupied by either a Magistrate or a judge, both bearers of standing legal status within the community, but the previously named rôles are standing *vis-à-vis* the given convened court. A sitting of a court is *ad hoc* itself, but similar relationships can exist with respect to a standing body, thus considerable flexibility can be achieved.

Let the term "*institution*" be used to refer to an *organization of at*

[14] *Vide* Chapter I, p. 14 ff.

least sufficient complexity to allow of status differences between its members. This excludes teams,[15] and primitive (standing) organizations. In virtue of their status certain individuals will have certain rights, duties and freedoms within the institutions of which they are members. In the case of a community-wide status and of status with respect to a certain code or a system of codes the regulations constitutive of the differences were formulated to apply to a certain type of contingency, whenever it arose within a certain area of activity. Where an institution is concerned the decisive regulations can have no such generality, and since they do not apply to any member of the community, but only to members of an institution as such, they are not general in application either. But they must have *within* the institution a generality isomorphic with the above, and for obvious reasons.

Institutional status of one member is strictly speaking specifically relative to the other members of the organization. Their status *vis-à-vis* the community is only one of: a member (rather than a non-member) of the given organization. Nonetheless if one is neither a member of the police force nor of a Masonic Lodge, then the fact that Joe Smith is the Chief Commissioner of Police is still of interest to him because that is a status significant for the community. But the fact that Joe Smith is also a Big Bellowing Bull in his Lodge is of no interest to him whatever. And yet it can be said that the Chief Commissioner of Police is a status within the Police Force much in the same way in which the Big Bellowing Bull is a status within the Masonic Lodge. Thus in some cases the possession of status within an institution seems to confer automatically some communal status, in other cases it does not; this needs further explanation.

Let us draw a distinction between a *public* and a *private* body;

(a) An organization shall be classified as *public* if it is devised to achieve *communal aims*. Clearly such a body will form part of the structure of the particular community, for it is devoted to the implementation of communal expectations, and thus has the same point as other communal arrangements. Naturally positions within such an organization are public, which is to say communal, and the status achieved by their members is of public interest.

It is possible to draw a distinction between at least two main types of public organization:

(i) An organization concerned directly with the working of the ma-

[15] I use the word "team" in a narrow technical sense, for in ordinary parlance we often say e.g. "They were a successful team for twenty years"; in my usage, a team is tran sient.

chinery of the community – a *social or public engineering organization*, for example, the Police Force, the legal institutions, the Parliament. In a typical case since such a body is the guardian of communal arrangements immediately relevant to almost every member of the community, the status people achieve in them is directly communal. Thus for example a constable of police has rights, etc. with respect to every citizen and could not carry out his duties unless he had. This should be qualified for while the remark seems clearly right with respect to some officials, it might be less convincing with respect to say a typist in the Police Headquarters, yet she has a status within this organization. To say that such positions keep the public body working and are thus communal is formalistic, and it is both more intuitive and more realistic to tie the automatic acquisition of a communal status to the direct relevance of the work done in the given position to the doings of an average citizen. Thus a constable will have a direct public status for obvious reasons, so will people concerned with directing the operations of a service organization; people concerned only with the internal workings of the organizations need not be regarded as having automatically a direct public status.

(ii) A service organization not concerned with the workings of a community but with achieving something on behalf of it, for example, the Commonwealth Shipping Lines, the Intelligence Service, and the Armed Forces. Here the status bearers have no more direct communal status than that of the members of Clubs and of commercial bodies, but in view of their importance they might have high secondary communal status. It should be noted that a service organization need not be less important or less essential than a social engineering organization – compare only the health service with the Board of Censors, the second unlike the first being a public engineering body is nonetheless far more dispensable than the first. Even though the distinction seems quite clear in principle, in many actual cases it might be far from clear how a given public organization should be classed.

(b) An *institution* shall be classified as *private* if it is designed to pursue aims that are not directly a matter of public or communal interest; typically it will be concerned with the interest of a select group within the community. Consequently positions and status within a private body are not a matter of direct public or communal interest. But, depending on the importance and standing of the body a secondary communal status might accrue to those who have status, particularly high status, within it. It might be the case that what such an institution achieves is *in fact* necessary for achieving purely communal aims – thus a drug company might produce what is indispensable to a public health scheme.

In practice even the main distinction cannot be kept neat. On the one side private organizations and enterprises can become so far-reaching that they come to be of public concern. The activities of the petrol companies and of some unions affect the community as a whole, and more significantly than say the public body controlling e.g. hunting seasons. Yet they do not cease to be private for this reason. An organization is private as long as it stays "independent" and continues to have its own narrow aims directed in principle at satisfying a selected group within the community, i.e. its own members – a group the membership of which is not determined by communal rules alone. But obviously the community might find it necessary to circumscribe and control both its activities and its membership. For instance, convicted felons might not be permitted to join certain organizations, and the aims of organizations can be limited by e.g. anti-trust laws. When the amount of such control is large the distinction specified above might become hard to apply. This might seem untidy but it is better that borderline cases should seem to be borderline, and that reasons for difficulties in characterizing a case should be apparent in the account given here.

Some organizations can be borderline in a different manner still, for it is possible for an organization to perform a public service and yet not to be directly a part of communal structure. Private telephone companies such as Bell's of the U.S.A., gas and electricity companies, etc. are often of this kind.[16] They would lose the r character if either they became direct communal instrumentalities or renounced the responsibility for the public service they accept and started to operate entirely for profit and the benefit of its members and/or shareholders.

Normally we say that a community *includes* a number of bodies, but that it is *composed of* or *consists of* smaller communities. That gives us a further indication of the nature of the difference between them. A community exists if and only if it is either separate or at least *in principle separable* from other groups, it is a sub-community with respect to another if it is not *independent* of it, i.e. forms part of its structure, and is dependent on the rules of the parent structure. Bodies are not separable from the parent community even in principle. We

[16] This is more directly a public service than the publicly important product of e.g. a drug co mpany mentioned.

cannot put, for example, the Police Force on its own and expect it, without a drastic change in its nature and organization, to act like a community and to fulfil the sort of rôle that must be and is assumed by a community.

But if we take East Gippsland and imagine the rest of Australia destroyed, it could continue to exist as a community. A number of adjustments will be necessary, e.g. in the new situation it cannot sell its produce outside, it cannot accept or demand financial assistance, it is not bound by policy rules of the Victorian Government and the Commonwealth Government, etc., but all these, though very important factors in the development, well-being and character of the existing community, are not what makes it a community, or this community.

There are groups that might cause some difficulty with separability as a criterion of community-hood.

There might be many other cases where the criterion of separability might be difficult to apply, for it is of course possible for any ties to arise among actual social structures.[17] These might not fit neatly into any paradigmatic construction, but such a construction is nonetheless necessary in order to render our thinking about the actual social structures more articulate and transparent.

[17] I take "social structure" to mean indiscriminately: group structure, sub-community, body, institution, etc. *Vide* also p. 111.

CHAPTER V

ELEMENTS OF THE ULTIMATE GROUP STRUCTURE

The previous chapters have established a number of concepts in terms of which it is possible to describe different interpersonal situations, and to state different views and theories concerning social and political phenomena. A community is what it is because it is composed of a number of individuals which inasmuch as they are members of this community, are capable of cooperation, and on a large scale, are capable of concerted action. This concerted action is possible if and only if in the group of individuals there exists a certain rule structure. All the other elements of importance to political and social discourse have to be viewed all the time as elements in terms of which this structure or organization which defined a community can be understood. The term "group structure" can be used to denote this organizational bond which exists between the members of the one community.

The importance of rules in this connection was sometimes questioned. For instance, R.M. Dworkin,[1] in denying that the system of law is a system of rules is committed to disagree with the general position outlined above. His examples of non-rule elements of law are principles and policies, e.g. (p. 35): "I call a 'policy' that kind of standard that sets out the goal to be reached, ... I call a 'principle' a standard that is to be observed, not because it will advance or secure an economic, political or social situation deemed desirable, but because it is a requirement of justice or fairness... Thus the standard that automobile accidents are to be decreased is a policy, and the standard that no man may profit by his own wrong a principle."

It will be clear that both policies and principles can be expressed in general rules to wit maxims; they were so expressed in the above quotation. It is however to be observed that Dworkin's view might be correct if allied to some narrower concept of a rule, where for instance each rule gives a specific prescription to specific persons. Such narrower

[1] "Is Law a System of Rules?."

interpretation leads to difficulties of demarcation to say the least, e.g. is "Render medical assistance when necessary" a rule or a standard? This is one of the reasons why it was not adopted here, but the main point is that it is only in the wider interpretation of "rule," as specified above, that I am disagreeing with Dworkin's view.

Members of a group will be members only inasmuch as they are involved in its group structure. Now there could be pre-communal groups, where there is some bond between members, but one which would not justify us in calling it a community. This will happen for instance if there exists no bond that connects all of the putative members together. A number of separate friendships between a number of separate individuals is not constitutive of a community, even if it might lead to one. But if friendships lead to overall cooperation some rudimentary structure will be discernible among these individuals. However the present concern is only with group structure of communities. I do not call this *communal structure* because to do so would tend to hide the fact that something very similar in terms of organizational bond can exist in groups that are *not* communities. In defining a community the existence of a common bond is not the only relevant desideratum.

The object of this chapter is to further our understanding of the nature of more sophisticated group structures. To see what basic types of sophistication are possible, and what types of sophisticated elements can stand in what kind of relation to each other. In doing this there is no intention of anticipating or of contradicting any empirical findings, but only of describing a category of elements and types of organizational features which can be discerned on purely conceptual and logical grounds and which might help to describe more clearly whatever can be found by empirical methods. "Sophisticated" refers here to sophisticated communities rather than to sophisticated groups, for a sub-communal group, such as a beehive, could be very complex from the point of view of a zoologist.

The sophistication that I have in mind comes about when relations between members of a community get beyond the stage of mere relations between individuals as such. In previous chapters some mention was made of sub-communities and sub-structures; now these can and do stand in relation to each other, consequently what belong to them stand not only in direct, but also in indirect relation to each other. E.g. John Doe and Richard Roe are not only related *qua* citizens but also as a director of one institution to the secretary of another, as a councillor of one shire to the visitor from another, etc. These relations introduce a whole new range of possibilities that can be, and often are, incorporated in communal structure. Some basic principles concerning these matters can be relatively easily discerned.

Let the term "body" denote a sub-structure, or an organization which is not a community; "institution", a body which involves the existence of standing positions within itself. Bodies and institutions form clusters whenever they stand in some definite relation to one another. Two bodies stand in definite relation to each other if the area of competence of one body limits the area of competence of the other, if whatever is achieved by one body is supported by what is achieved by the other, or if one body has an effect opposite to the other, or limits it.

One body or institution *limits* another if the possibility of effective institutional action of one institution is determined by the other. Thus, a Court of Appeals limits the competence of the Lower Court, for the decisions of the Lower Court stand if and only if they are not contravened by the Court of Appeals. A cultural exchange organization or a scientific body may have its activity limited by a security organization, etc.

One institution will *support* another if the activity of one is made possible or carried out or taken up by the other. Thus a Police Force or a Sheriff's Office supports a Court if it carries out its decision to have people arrested, kept in custody or released. The Department of External Affairs can support the Department of Trade if it takes action which is calculated or designed to make the achievement of the ends of the Department of Trade easier.

An institution is *opposing* another institution if and only if the aims of both of the institutions cannot be achieved or cannot be fully achieved at the same time. Thus any success on the part of the Dunlop Rubber Company limits the success that can be had by the Goodyear Rubber Company, provided that the aim of each of these organizations is to corner the entire car tyre market.

As long as we speak only of clusters, neither the aims nor the scope of the particular sub-structures are dovetailed purposely in order to achieve a common effect. Thus the relations are factual and largely accidental, depending on the aims of the organizations as well as on their concrete situation. If these have completely different aims they cannot affect each other. If they operate in separate areas, and sometimes when what they want to achieve is of such a nature that no success by one can affect the potential success of others, as for example is the case with clubs dedicated to keeping their own members physically fit, they still do not affect each other even if they have identical aims. A cluster arises when bodies are forced into either competition or cooperation. It will be clear that the need of a better definition of such relations will be forcibly drawn to the attention of those who belong to the organizations in question. However if this requirement were to be fulfilled the kind of structure would normally change.

The type of relation that usually emerges in such cases is determined by formal rules. Relations between: Courts and the Police Force; Department of Trade and the Department of External Affairs, etc. are of this kind. Here rules determine formally their relative competence; for example, the Court cannot arrest anybody because it is not an enforcement authority. It has the right to determine who ought to be kept in custody or arrested, and the enforcement authority has not only the right, but a duty, to see that those decisions are carried out, but cannot decide such matters in its own right. These rules regulate their respective spheres of competence and determine how they are to be dovetailed. Let a "system of sub-structures" denote this type of set-up, in contradistinction to a mere cluster of bodies and/or institutions on the one hand, and to a system of rules and/or codes on another.

A system of sub-structures is in some respects very much like a community whose members are institutions or bodies, and sometimes committees. Those member institutions will have some duties, rights and privileges *qua* institutions. In the system they will usually have different status with respect to each other. The status of a Court of Appeals is different from the status of the Court of Petty Sessions, or from the status of the Police Force, and so on. Since there can be several Courts of Petty Sessions, more than one institution can have similar status. But since institutions are not individuals, each of them consists of members and those will have some status within their respective institutions. This is not equivalent to a status directly within the system *qua* system, but this type of status position is also possible. The Governor or the sovereign obviously has status within the system as such if he has the right to appoint judges, to grant clemency, etc. Generally such a person will have multiple status. For example, whoever is the Supreme Judge has certain primary rights, duties and privileges in virtue of this position within the institution, e.g. the Supreme Court. He may have certain rights directly in the system and enjoy a status within it similar to the status that an institution could have. Suppose that a Court, i.e. an institution, decides that a certain person should be detained. A Chief Constable, i.e. a person, has to issue an order for his apprehension, but he need not be a member of any institution which is a member of the legal system. He may hold the position directly within the system, and then has a status, i.e. duties, rights and privileges with respect to the system, but not internally with respect to any of the member institutions. For him the system is like an institution of which he is a member, and the other members might be institutions. Double status is possible for e.g. a judge, in addition to his status at the courts, might possess also an independent status similar to that of the Chief Constable. Independent status of another kind is also possible. It would arise if e.g. being a judge determined what actual positions in legal institutions should be accorded to the given individual if he is to be a member of them.

Further it is possible to be a member of more than one institution within a system, e.g. to be a Director of more than one company, a member of more than one club. This can lead to what could be called a composite status. For a Director of half a dozen companies, and a member of several clubs, etc., could become important in the community, for that reason alone, and this can be recognized in many ways. Importantly it can manifest itself in this individual having some rights, duties and privileges within the system, but need not. If it did those would be straight-out rights, duties and privileges within the system, but dependent on the composite status of the individual in question, the composite status in itself being the sum total of all his rights, etc. within the several separate bodies, etc. as such.

Status within a system, due to membership of certain bodies, will naturally depend very much on the status of the bodies themselves. Thus the picture grows in complexity. Further complications, for example in terms of clusters of systems, and systems of systems, could be discerned, however there is but little profit in producing in detail all the logically possible complexities in isolation from practice. The trend of things is clear anyway. We may add that when we talk of bodies, institutions and systems, or systems of systems of bodies and institutions, we come to the point where we have the ultimate structure of which they are elements. It is important to observe that there must be such an ultimate structure in each case. Let us think back to the distinction between a body[2] and a community. By definition a body cannot control more than a section of the individual's life, it is therefore depen-

[2] Here I am going to use "body" to stand for: body, institution, organization and *vice versa*. I shall adhere to this loose usage whenever economy of words demands it.

dent on other controls to be able to fulfil its function(s). This can be achieved in one or two ways: (a) There are other bodies or systems of bodies that jointly take care of this. But then they are not independent of the institution in question, since they support it and make it possible. In fact there could often be more control than necessary for this purpose, but there must be at least enough to make the whole workable. The structure that provides this is then in either case the ultimate structure; or (b) all the other rules are direct communal rules, and the institution(s) or system(s) in question are the only one(s) of their kind. But then the institution and the community together form the necessary structure, which is ultimate, and is a community, as indeed was the other one as well. These facts could be easily obscured. For instance it will be clear that there is no ultimate world-body. On the other hand, what look like ultimate bodies are not completely independent. Thus neither Britain, Australia, Poland, the U.S.A., nor the U.S.S.R. can claim total independence from other states. One might be tempted to say that there are structural concentrations – strong, but not ultimate social systems, forming together an untidy common system, but failing to form an ultimate structure.

This view is mistaken; no one denies links, they do exist fortunately, but they are not always the right type of link, and there are not enough of them. As has been argued above, a communal structure needs to be based on rules, whether general or diversified between bodies and sub-communities, sufficient in their totality to inform on the whole the lives of its members. A sub-communal group is also structured but the links provided are insufficient to determine what a safe and reasonable action would be for its members in a sufficient number of types of case. Members have to fend for themselves in many important aspects of their lives.

Consequently an institution or organization presupposes a community for it needs to rely on otherwise promoted *modus vivendi* among the people among whom it operates, *not all of whom are its members.* This last is important, for if a group of people bind together to achieve a common aim *vis-à-vis* declared strangers, where all non-members of this group are such strangers, they, like Plato's band of robbers, become a social group whose function is community-like, since it is only in terms of membership of this group that the individuals are not on their own. They must provide rules for at least some minimal *modus vivendi* to operate between themselves *qua* members of the "organization" for the simple reason that it cannot be important from elsewhere. Where there is a *modus vivendi* there is at least a budding community. Where there is no effective *modus vivendi* only sporadic and fragmented cooperation is possible. A body, and specially an institution, as it was specified above, is too sophisticated to exist where there is only fragmented cooperation, for an institution requires the existence of status differences. This is not to say that at pre-communal stages there could not exist relatively loose association of individuals, but only that these could not be structured enough to qualify as an organization. Clearly then the ultimate structure with respect to: bodies, systems of bodies and/or institutions, etc., will always be their respective community.

Where different communities have links, they either are, or are not, joined into one larger community. They are not so joined if: (a) the links are predominantly between communal groups rather than individuals; (b) the ground level rules are largely independent of each other, e.g. what is legal in one case is a crime in another; (c) all the direct authorities[3] *vis-à-vis* individuals are particular community, e.g. State orientated. Thus it is impossible to be a citizen of the United Nations as such, but possible to be a citizen of the U.S. with the British Commonwealth providing an in-between case – contrast here passport regulations with the position of Privy Council, etc. An ultimate structure as understood here is the ultimate overall community from the point of view of the individuals concerned. Characteristically separate and independent communities even when inter-connected may adopt contrary or opposing ways of life, provided only that they have agreed on all *external modi vivendi* operating between groups, e.g. States, as such. When in Rome do as the Romans do, is a type of inter-community rule suitable for the purpose. It will be clear that on this test Poland, Australia, etc., are in fact separate communities not sub-communities of, say, the United Nations, which is not to say that hard to decide cases cannot be found in plenty.

The fact that the ultimate structure must comprise a single community could be concealed by the variety it might permit between the styles of its component bodies and communities, for in a varied, sophisticated and large system, the rules dealing with matters concerning everybody in the whole state tend to be very general. Thus building regulations are passed by lesser bodies to suit local conditions, but the criminal law tends to be state-wide, since it does not depend on local conditions. In many matters sub-communities may be granted complete autonomy. But this autonomy *is granted,* that is, it is either left

[3] This will be discussed later.

or guaranteed by the rules of the system and it will be curbed if it endangers the working of the whole. What is more, the sub-unit is understood to be one, it works as a part of the system, and unless the whole structure changes it must be the system that imposes limits on its sub-communities and not *vice versa*.

In the case of independent communities, the links are between them as such, and there are no direct links between individuals coming from different units. An Englishman is partner of a citizen of Denmark in the way in which a Londoner is a partner in common enterprise with a man from Glasgow, but neither is the neighbour of the other, while the second pair only are fellow citizens. This demarcation line is neither hard nor fast. In Australia, the states often have delusions of being the ultimate social systems. Some of us might have the delusion that the Common Market is the ultimate system in Western Europe; both are wrong, but there could be many hard to decide cases.

One possible criterion of the independence of a community lies in the way in which common decisions are taken and the levels on which they are binding. In the Commonwealth of Australia, the decisions of the Commonwealth Government override those of a State Government on Commonwealth matters, even where these have to be carried out within the State concerned. In the United Nations, on the contrary, it is the decision of each particular state that is binding on its citizens and it cannot be overridden by the United Nations. At worst United Nations membership can be denied to a state and external sanctions applied to it. The first is a single state, the second an alliance. It can be said provisionally that the State is the ultimate political community. To this it might be very well objected that people who do not belong to the same State can still have some sort of bond between them or accept the same rules of behaviour, which appears very similar to the bonds that exist between members of a community, and are formed by community of arrangements. But these bonds are essentially accidental, or due to cultural, etc. similarities, independent of communal structure. Basically it is the case that the different e.g. states have independently developed similar rules. This by the way is not to deny interaction, but only to deny direct influence by imposition of common expectations. A fashion, even if important, is not a rule.

A community exists if and only if interindividual bonds have formed that are sufficiently important to affect the lives of the members of the community to a critical extent. A criterion of whether a group is a community can be found in the fact that it is not possible to give a satisfactory explanation of somebody's circumstances, and I mean circumstances in the widest possible sense, without mentioning that he is a member of this or that community, if he belongs to one. Thus a life of Copernicus not saying that he was a Pole, a life of Garibaldi not saying that he was an Italian, a life of Marco Polo, not saying that he was a Venctian, etc. would be seriously faulty for the story of the man in question would be grossly incomplete. Being a member of a particular community is one of the most important facts about a person. This is not the sort of importance where it may be important to me that I have won a tennis tournament, it may be important to you that you belong to a bridge club, etc. This lesser kind of importance depends entirely on the person's attitude to winning a tournament or belonging to a bridge club. In short they are important because they are regarded as important. But being an Australian or an Englishman is inescapably important, for it has nothing to do with one's interest or belief whether or not one is entitled to certain legal protections, whether one has certain rights, whether one has certain duties, and whether obedience to certain laws will be enforced on one whether one likes it or not, and this is a decisive difference. A community is based in a relationship that perforce determines things which are objectively important in one's conduct. Thus we have rules which make it possible for one to pursue one's interests, rules which determine the way in which one has to do it, rules wich give one different types of security, etc. One cannot help but organize one's life in reference to such rules, especially if the set is relatively complete. But most of the things most people have to face in life are totally unaffected by their belonging to say the international Philatelists' Association. There is no *need* for *it* to have any but isolated and fragmentary influence on their life. Membership of a community or a state is a way of life, membership of a tennis club is an interest, and membership of a commercial company might be a job. This argument is of course concerned with effective rather than legal membership of a community. So a nominal Swiss citizen who lived sixty consecutive years in Sweden is for this purpose a citizen, or what might be called a permanent resident of Sweden. His legal status can give him a special position in the Swedish community, though it need not. Here again the very complex problem of possible relations between a community and an individual becomes important. Clearly in view of the possible complexities the above offers only very general guidelines, but they are no less useful for being general and open textured.

One can have a cluster of *independent* social and communal structures i.e. communities, but not a system of them. Thinking of organizations we can say that a community may comprise a number of bodies which form systems, systems of systems and lastly an ultimate system of bodies which is the community in question. But this of course is not the only type of complexity possible. We can distinguish also interconnected sub-communities, that is, structures that deserve the name of a community even though they are part of and constitutive of a greater one. While we are saying this, it will be well to remember that the two types of complexity can and usually do go together, though it is not logically necessary that they should. It seems to be a practical necessity however on any level of sophistication.

Normally we say that a community *includes* a number of bodies, but we say that it *is composed of* or *consists of* smaller communities. This gives us an indication of the difference. If a community consists in a number of smaller communities, these *dependent* structures may form systems, clusters, and systems of systems of communities.

Let us return to the main point. I have cited separability as a criterion of community-hood. But there are groups that might cause us some difficulty with this. I have in mind things like the Jewish community in Tsarist Russia, or the East Indian community in London. These live intermingled with other people, and quite obviously the set of communal rules that applies to them *qua* members of a social group in which they live are general, not Indian or Jewish, rules. So it would seem that they are not communities at all in the primary sense which we are investigating in this study. Still we can think of them as separable – there are sufficient customary, religious, etc. rules in operation among these groups to enable them to have a separate communal existence as such. This is a difficult matter to decide, but in principle one would be able to say that were it to become independent such a group would have to make a much bigger adjustment than say the community of Northern Ireland. At the very least, it would have either to adopt as their own, or substitute for, a number of regulations, that up to the point of separation directed a large proportion of their lives. We might say that here we have a vanishing point of sub-community, but a terminological decision seems of little enough importance, and the problem can be left, having been noted.

The separability of communities will impose limitations and determine what ties can exist between them even if they form an overall unit. Quite clearly the existence of one community can put limitations on what another community can do. We have an example of that where communities have territorial claims and enforce regulations over the territories which they call their own. Someone residing in a territory external to the given community belongs then of necessity to another community and our rules and regulations *cannot* apply to him.

The question arises whether all ultimate independent communities are states and if not what is the character of a state? It could be easily claimed that a state is simply the focal point of all the communal bonds of all its members. But this alone is not sufficient to define a state. Many primitive tribes, for example in Northern Australia, can be regarded as being communities who at least at some times owed no allegiance to anybody, had no bonds with any other community, and were in short the ultimate communal structure, from the point of view of their members, yet they were not states. Nor will a simple addition of territorial sovereignty do. For if such tribes lived on separate islands in the South Seas, defended their territories and had a conception of different islands belonging to different tribes, they still would not be states.

Thus one is driven towards the view that a state must display a certain minimum degree of organizational sophistication. It is extremely difficult to say what this degree should be. There are of course quite clear cases: (a) A community composed of a reasonably large number of individuals, but containing no sub-communities, no public institutions and no public positions, very clearly fails to be a state; (b) A large complex community composed of various sub-communities, some of them containing further sub-communities, whose structure consists *inter alia* of specialised public organization and bodies, such as the Army, the Police Force, the Parliament, the Cabinet, etc., very clearly is a state.

But between these two extremes many doubtful cases are possible. Some could be found existing in more primitive ages. But in more primitive conditions we might very well be tempted to count as a state what would be a doubtful candidate, or even no candidate at all were it to exist at present. In other words it might be that the application of the word "state" is relative to the importance and sophistication of the community *vis-à-vis* other independent communities much like *a city* is.

The term "state" as commonly employed is often tied to concepts such as territorial and/or social sovereignty, which were shown above to be inadequate. We also tend to talk of the national state, but it is clear that non-national states are possible, that national boundaries can exceed state boundaries, and *vice versa.*

The term "state" is used in contra-distinction to "Tribe"; "Community"; "Village," etc. where these refer to ultimate group structures as happens when people are said to live in villages, and no more, when they form isolated communities, or are organized in tribes. Tribes, villages and separate communities are self-governing and form single separate units; in this they are like states. It could be suggested that a state differs from them for (a) it is a political unit, and (b) it has a central government.

(a) Being a political unit is a matter of relative sophistication, of which more will be said later. We do not talk of *political* actions taking place on primitive levels. Thus a New Guinea village has no politics, though it has: aims, customs, and even its own territory.

(b) The question of the existence of a central government brings in a number of further considerations. Each community, not only a State, must have a common authority and a common set of rules that apply to all, but it is only where there are alternative authorities and allegiances that we are justified in talking of government or central government. This is in fact only possible where there are some sub-communities and possibly also communal organizations, nor will the term "Central Government" apply unless these sub-structures are either numerous enough or strong enough to provide, at least in theory, a possible alternative to it.

The upshot of this line of reasoning is that states are centrally organized, relatively complex, and sophisticated systems of (sub) communities.

This is of course rather imprecise, and leaves many unanswered questions, e.g. is it necessary for a state to have the sole control over a well defined territory? It seems to me at least possible to argue that it is not. But it is reasonably clear that we call something a state largely in recognition of actual features which are difficult, if not impossible, to tabulate in advance.

We have said that the final community must be independent and must have sufficient scope to provide sufficient background for its members to organize their lives on this basis. If this suffices you may say that one exists, whether or not it has any specific territory which it calls its own, provided only that it has the scope and sovereignty required. Further, there is no reason to suppose that a number of nomadic tribes could not form an overall tribal structure, that is, an ultimate community. This type of structure does not demand that the community should have territorial sovereignty. I mention this point because the contrary is often enough assumed without argument, especially if the word "state" is used to describe the ultimate community.

Having said this much I propose to leave the term "state" as an ordinary non-technical term to be applied by feel, and without serious theoretical commitment as is usually done in ordinary discourse. This method will at least preserve its attractive vagueness.

Communities *qua* communities: – can have similar aims and a common policy; they can have conflicting aims and conflicting policies; also they can have similar or conflicting interests. Thus communities may limit each other, support each other and oppose each other. Here it is not necessary to refer to any actions that such communities might take, but only to the way in which they are set up, which of course will take effect in single and communal action, that will follow the pattern determined by the respective structure in each case.

Communities will form a cluster whenever they are in contact with each other, have common or opposing interests, aims and policies. But they will form a common structure, if, and only if, their common and conflicting spheres of interest, aims, policies and interests are dovetailed in an orderly manner. There must be inter-communal rules according to which conflicts and agreements can resolve themselves. These rules can apply to actions by individuals and/or to actions by communities. In these terms there are three possibilities. In order to have a consistent terminology, if the structural rules apply only to actions by communities we shall say that these communities are *federated;* if the rules apply to both we shall say that these are *sub-communities forming a larger overall unit;* if they apply only to actions of individuals the structure will be held to revert to a *single homogeneous community.* These points are to be taken to apply only to the actions of putative communities; bodies and organizations are expressly excluded, thus they can exist in a homogeneous community.

In these terms we can distinguish a further difference between the bodies and communities belonging to a bigger unit. If bodies form a cluster, if they have conflicting and common competence, interests, policies and aims, this alone will tend to show that they belong to one communal structure, and if they do, partly determine it. This is not true about communities: they can be independent but bodies are not separable from their communities, thus it is in terms of their effect on the community that their working is to be understood. Therefore only bodies in one community can affect each other.

There is another obvious possibility *viz.* communities that do affect each other might fail to have links and agreements in terms of rules, then they are independent of each other and fail to have co-operative agreements with each other. Clearly between federation and this state of affairs there can be discerned many intermediate stages, but all of them comprise at the very least clusters of communities.

To be careful we should say that this question might be out of place in a very simple situation, for instance where there is some organised and relatively sophisticated co-operation, but perhaps as yet neither the concept of sub-community nor a concept of an organization can get a grip.

The picture that we have painted is that past the relatively unsophisticated stage at which no sub-groups are established, the group structure can develop in two different ways, both in terms of substructures. *Firstly,* the sub-structures can be communities in their own right and can form a larger unit along the lines indicated above. *Secondly,* the sub-structures can be just organizations, which are not communities but nevertheless act as discernible units within the parent community and affect its character. Since bodies are not separable from their communities, it is in terms of their effect on the community that their working is to be understood. This has to be qualified as for instance an oil company can have conflicting or common interests across many different independent communities. But then they have links in only one sphere, that of marketing of oil products. But marketing itself is limited by security, political and legal rules instituted within the communities in which the company operates. There is international law, and there are agreements between nations, but rules thus instituted are dependent on enforcement by member nations, and work through them. If for instance an international law against misleading advertising exists it is only effective on those states that accept it.[4] There is no process of law that can ensure compliance in the absence of state-enforcement, though a boycott could do it, but a boycott need not make any reference to any laws and/or rules. Thus rules exceeding states and other ultimate communal units are composite and secondary in character, the formula being: "In states *a*, *b*, *c* (or all states) it is required that all marketing bodies do *X* in accordance with international rule *RX*". In absence of any rules on state level including the absence of "sustaining" rules, an organization cannot exist, though the existence of a community sustains the possibility of maintaining such projects within it. In some

[4] The truth of this dictum is amply illustrated by the U.N. rule of equal pay for equal work.

cases of course arrangements can be both primitive and rudimentary. It could be objected that even if we have no community we can have co-operation, at least sporadic cooperation. Why then not an organization based on this kind of relationship? If an organization must rest on standing arrangements, these too are prior to communities.

Since sub-communities are separable, a link between them must be explicitly and separately provided because the possibility of common policies, aims, actions, etc., can rest securely on this alone. Any tie between communities over and above the casual relationship requires explanation, as was the case with individuals, and for similar reasons. It must be an explanation that will show how a number of communities are capable of concerted action, common policy, and a common structure. Rule structure joining separable communities will then be roughly on the model of the rule structure joining separate individuals. It is not strictly necessary to have special arrangements for the existence of bodies in a community simply because they cannot help being integrated in terms of the communal rules belonging to the community in which they operate; however some of the rules *can* be specially directed at bodies and/or institutions and can deal with their mutual relations as such. It is also possible for sub-communal bodies to form an overall organization, and have a sub and ultimate unit structure. I do not mean to say that regulations between bodies are impossible or do not exist, on the contrary. All I want to stress is that they need not exist for those bodies to form elements of the community. Nor do I wish to deny that relationships between bodies are formal, some of them must be, otherwise we could not talk of systems of bodies at all, for if they all belong to one system, their relations must be orderly.

The question becomes: can a formally organized body involving standing rules be the only structure of this order? In absence of sustaining arrangements such as a monetary system, or something comparable, a system of ownership, etc., there could not exist for instance a marketing organization for these are among the arrangements that are presupposed by any organized marketing activity. But, if the marketing body tried to provide all the background necessary for its activity it would tend to become a community in its own right, *viz.* a lot more than just a commercial enterprise.

A candidate for a counter-example must be primitive enough to require less background than is provided by a communal structure.

The simplest case would be an organization requiring no background at all. This might be provided by a band of men travelling in a caravan bartering with disorganized individuals along the route. The people with whom they barter need not form a community, but they need to *have* something worth bartering. This alone does not prove that they need a concept of ownership: physical possession is sufficient. But the men in the caravan need a fair amount of organization, they need leadership and rules of behaviour sufficient to provide for concerted action adequate to achieve their objective. Security, cohesion and united front *vis-à-vis* other people would be absolutely necessary. These cannot be had unless sufficient peace among them, food, clothing, shelter and a system of defence are provided. If the caravan is the only thing that provides all these things, i.e. it is not an extension of a greater community applying this community's rules, it itself will come under the definition of community as given above, for its scope will be sufficient to provide the main framework for the lives of its members.

This is true assuming that the band of individuals in question is reliably organized, i.e. that its members can rely on each other in a sufficient number of relevant respects. Should the envisaged situation be more primitive than that then the question asked is out of place. For there might be still some cooperation left but neither the concept of a community nor a concept of an organization could be properly applied.

In one good sense community and/or organization must be separate from all other structured units even if it is a part of a larger whole. In this latter case it might be objected that there is no separation for the rules and administrative machinery of the supra-structure constitute and control the others. However they cannot do it in complete detail or the sub-structures would lose all identity and the whole would become homogeneous.

This is best illustrated by taking two units of the same order, e.g. two cities belonging to one State. Each will have to control similar aspects of the lives of their members, and have rules concerned e.g. with: building, garbage collection, maintenance of public property, shopping, etc., otherwise the scope of each would be insufficient to call it a community. At least some of the rules must be distinct or it would be impossible to discern more than one unit. These need not be rules controlling people's behaviour directly, e.g. building regulations, but can be secondary. Thus even if Vienna and Innsbruck had identical first order rules, a Viennese would have to appeal to a different authority for his building permit than an Innsbruckian. This constitutes a crucial difference, and would not be affected even if the character of the building rules was in fact determined by the Australian government.

Two rules are different if they are inconsistent, opposed or simply require different, though not opposed, actions. But as the above example shows, they can be different even if they require identical performance provided only that they spell out different allegiances. For if in certain matters A and B have to follow the directions of different Town Clerks, Councils, etc., then even if the directions are identical A and B belong to different organizations (communities in this case). One cannot have two different final authorities in the same matter on any given level, thus one is forced to belong to one and no more than one unit of the given order. But there are many exceptions to this. To begin with organizations concerned with different pursuits can be joined by the same individuals. Secondly, one's allegiance can be split temporally or subject matter-wise. One can move from place to place at intervals and own property in more than one state, and these are only the most obvious complications. Notwithstanding all this, communities are each designed to act as a whole, and each must have a certain rule-gestalt and rule cohesion, and this imposes a limitation on how many of its citizens can have how many split allegiances. For it is obvious that if the majority of its members owed their main relevant allegiance elsewhere, the unit so constituted would hardly be a viable community.

Basically then at any given time any individual is a member of one community. This had to be qualified, for split allegiance is possible, but this in turn requires qualification. A split allegiance is in principle possible only by default or as it were on borrowed time for whenever there are two genuinely different and *independent* communities there can always arise a conflict of interest, as it can as a matter of fact also happen in the case of two institutions, etc. If it happens the individual will have to choose his primary allegiance. It is possible to prevaricate in a multitude of ways but the issue is in principle always there and if it arises in fact one citizenship only can be chosen for obvious reasons.

It can be objected that an organization within a community can have interests conflicting with the interests of this community, and Mr. Nader has provided us with many an example. The reply is that in this case there is no difficulty in principle for the allegiances are of a different order – the allegiance to one's community, e.g. a state, always takes precedence over the allegiance to an organization, institution or body. It has to be remembered that this is a purely political and not a moral or religious claim, and also that these differing types of claims can clash.

Often a semblance of membership of more than one community can be created where the individual in question has no more than the status of an outsider or guest in the other community or communities; it will be then helpful to investigate this type of position.

The main point of the outsider's status, even though there are any number of different standings that an outsider can have in a community, is this: communal rules do not apply to him in the way in which they apply to full members of the community. Of course we know that a visitor has to expect to have to follow the laws of the country, and if an Englishman goes to Germany he cannot go on driving on the left-hand side of the road. This is part of the necessary *rules for admission of visitors*. They specify the relation between the visitors and the community in which he is a visitor. Since the Germans drive on the right-hand side of the road, visitors to Germany have to do so as well. A visitor follows certain rules that are imposed by a body of which he is not a member. This relation is on an essentially temporary basis. The fact that he finds it easier to drive on the left-hand side is irrelevant to the rule structure of the community which he is visiting. But the members of the community are involved in the structure, not only in the capacity of following the rules, but also in somehow determining or influencing the rules.

Let us illustrate this point. Suppose there is a small community which has some peculiar regulations. Out of respect for their gods they observe an hour of complete silence between noon and 1.00 p.m. and all shops close to make the observance complete. A stranger holidaying there has to follow this rule. If this community consisted of two hundred people and at some stage there were one thousand visitors on that island, then even though the people then resident on the island would stand 5/1 against this rule, this would constitute no reason to change it. If however it was five members of the island community who would have thought that this rule is unnecessary and uncongenial against one of its supporters, then there would be the best possible reason for deleting it. This explains to a large extent why many countries are so very much stricter in admitting immigrants than visitors. In a way this is the sort of reason traditionally given for the White Australia Policy – the influx of the other people will affect our way of life. Admittedly tourists affect the Italian way of life, but in a different way.

Notwithstanding the above arguments it is clear that one can be conjointly a member of an ultimate community, and some of its sub-communities in descending order. Thus if A is the ultimate community, B its sub-community and C a sub-community of B, one can be a citizen of A, B and C at the same time.

If a community consists of smaller component communities, then there has to be a set of rules concerning those component communities requiring that all be in concert. There will have to be some procedure for determining the aims and policies of the higher level community, some means of checking on whether the rules are observed and implemented (where need be) in sub-communities, some means of enforcing the decisions, and so on.

Nevertheless component i.e. sub-communities must have a structure of their own which is at least semi-independent, to this is *added* the top-level supra-community structure. Many complexities can now arise, for instance, it will be clear that the type of action of which a component community is capable depends on its structure. Consequently the sub-structure involves *inter alia* status differences, that matter on the higher level. For what is required of the component community cannot be carried out until they are recognised. Thus for instance, Town Clerks *qua* Town Clerks of their respective towns will be responsible on the higher level for having certain regulations observed. Thus this position nominally limited to a sub-group becomes significant beyond this limit. Quite as obviously, there could be positions where the membership of this rather than that sub-community would be quite irrelevant; for example: the President of a state; the Commander of the Armed Forces, etc. The membership of a lesser body makes those people citizens of the state as such and this is all that matters. There will be a sliding scale between these two types, with some cases quite hard to decide.

Importantly state, or ultimate community orientated positions, whether they apply to individuals or to groups of individuals, are a *conditio sine qua non* of the existence of a sophisticated composite group-structure, short of this there can be no authorities to deal with matters arising on the ultimate level. If a system has no status positions then it is obviously limited and primitive. If status positions exist in sub-communities, they could form a more or less loose association, but not a bigger component community unless it has similar sophistication. For it is unconceivable that the ultimate body, the pinnacle of the structure, should not be able to deal with matters as efficiently or at the very best on a level as sophisticated as its parts. This is not to say that it is better equipped to deal with every kind of matter – some are better dealt with on the levels at which they arise – thus sub-communities and organizations are needed, but unless the state is to be an anachronism or a liablity, it must be as well if not better equipped to deal with matters of its appropriate kind.

It is essential also to the higher-order unit being a community, that everybody ought to have, in his own right, some status with respect to the ultimate structure. The least one can have is of course the position of a citizen i.e. a member of this community.

To this could be objected on the ground that a number of communities might each have the membership of the overall community, that people with certain special status in member communities could have state orientated positions in virtue of this; that people who have certain status within a body or organization might have a status, duties, rights and privileges on the level of overall organization while no one has a position on the level of the higher organization for any other reason at all. In such circumstances rank and file citizens of the sub-community would have no general community status whatever.

This is possible but it is a significantly different form of organization, i.e. a federation of communities. The clearest case of federation exists when all the overall rules deal with relations between communities and none with relations between individuals. Then federal positions, if any, can only be significant on the general level, and the rules of the federation alone are basically insufficient as community rules. Between this and the typical single community however complex there are many possible intermediate steps which I shall not consider. The European Common Market affords a good example of this organizational form. It would not be conducive to clarity to have the same name for a federation and a supra-community for the different names distinguish between a single community and a relatively loose association of communities. Where a single community is concerned we noted at least two types of complication and diversity: *One* in terms of sub-structures or organizations; *the other* in terms of sub-communities. Where a federation is concerned the diversity is obvious, and we need an account of the unity between its members, this too is to be given in terms of rules albeit less tight than in the previous case, and notably on a lesser scope.

To recapitulate, we have mentioned that the supra-community has to have its own rules for it must be capable of concerted actions. Nonetheless sub-communities have some independence, that is in as far as the sub-community rules are competent there is no need for rules on the level of the higher order community to deal with some matters. It is further the case that at least some bodies within a community might enjoy a measure of independence in that they are the judge of their actions within certain limits. For instance they might be able to impose rules in those areas where the citizens of the community are left freedom by the community. Thus a state might leave one the freedom to decide how to attempt to sell a book yet if one becomes a salesman for the Encyclopaedia Britannica, one has to follow strictly an involved and precisely indicated sales procedure. Also of course, such organizations can have something sub-communal like by-laws. For instance, to take again the traffic regulations, the traffic code may specify the maximum speed permitted on the road and it may specify what rest periods drivers of trucks must have, but a rule of a road-hauling company may specify lesser maximum speeds and larger maximum rest periods and in this way they will, within the limits, impose their own regulations to implement the rules of the road in a way binding only the members of this particular body.

Where sub-communities are concerned the lesser units have the full, or almost the full range of communal arrangements, but these are limited by the rules of the higher order unit. Thus if in the ultimate community there is a general law against vendetta, this cannot be a permitted part of the way of life of one of the sub-communities. Sometimes a sub-community can disregard this and act against the ultimate unit, e.g. the persistent attachment of Corsicans to vendetta. This imposes a strain on the ultimate group structure, but within limits it can be borne. When there are multiple areas of strain there must come a point where the "lesser unit" cannot be regarded as a sub-community, but at best as a colony. In this connection let us observe that a number of rules, common between the sub-unit and the ultimate structure, could be and in fact must be *adopted as their own* by members of the sub-community if there is to exist a genuine ultimate community. If there are no such rules (or not a sufficient number of them), it would be proper to say that the larger body imposes its will on the lesser one, or occupies it, which is a different relation. No ultimate community could possibly consist entirely of its own colonies, for quite obviously it would lack cohesion, and real ability to act as an overall unit.

The ultimate structure as here described, though it has some rules of its own, is not something over and above its component units, it consists in them. Further, members of the supra-community belong to it in their own right. They can do so only if they have internalized its rules, i.e. if they accept communal expectations on this level as positive reasons for acting. Should this fail there are only three possibilities left: (a) Individuals do not act on these rules at all; in this case there is on ultimate structure; (b) Individuals act on these rules in so far and because they are institutionalised in their own particular sub-units. This is obviously a federation of communities, a discernibly different and less cohesive form of structure; (c) The sub-unit is a colony of the other power. In this case an individual need not be a citizen of the colonial power *qua* being a citizen of the colony. He need not, and seldom does, give his allegiance to the colonial power. Thus if *per impossibile* the colonial power were to consist entirely of its colonies it would have citizens of its own, and no one, or almost no one, would be loyal to it. This is an obviously impossible situation for it effectively excludes the possibility of the existence of communal expectations on this level. If an actual state approaches this condition it is ripe for a revolution or a civil war.

It thus becomes important to be able to know when individuals genuinely accept the rules of this, that or another group. One can suggest two tests:

(a) Most simply – *whether members of the sub-unit observe these rules as rules or simply avoid consequences of disobedience.* (Think of acting contrary to the rules when not being observed; of willingness to admit it or to boast to other members of one's own circle, etc. For example, many schoolboys do not behave like citizens of their schools.)
(b) At a deeper level, more difficult to assess, *whether members of the sub-unit see themselves as bound by the rules*, that is, regard themselves as obligated to follow them. This can be expressed by saying that the citizens have internalised the rules.

It has to be remembered that: (i) we often enough break rules even when we genuinely accept them (as lots of people do with marriage vows), and (ii) we can follow rules we do not accept in a fair semblance of the genuine performance, for all sorts of reasons: timidity, fear of informants (as in Orwell's *1984*), etc. Thus test (b) is concerned with the point of the distinction. Test (a) is sufficient as a preliminary test, but can be regarded as showing in effect that a b-type state of affairs either exists or not, and therefore does not specify an independent criterion as such.

The above findings can then be expressed by saying that if condition (b) applies to a sufficient proportion of the rules that are the formal bond between the ultimate and the sub-community, the sub-unit is a part of the higher order community. If this is not the case the relation between the two units is a relation between two separate communities or groups in one of the many possible forms.

This applies easily to clear-cut cases, like "the Greater London" and "England" on the one hand, and "Germany" and "Poland" during the Second World War, on the other. But generally there are large possibilities of complication. There could be gradation (for example, this is to a large extent a separate community), or incomplete inclusion (for example, this community is independent in such and such a respect, for example education or taxation, and some others). Equally clearly the fact that in this or that case the relation is not clear-cut is not tantamount to an imperfection or lack of sophistication.

Let us observe that in a complex community, there will exist a double interaction between the community and organizations within it.

On the one hand the sub-communities, institutions, bodies and organizations, be they religious, commercial or others, will determine to some extent the gestalt of the community, and will make a significant difference to the community's group structure. They impose a large number of by-laws, and supplementary rules. Codes will come into existence which determine the behaviour of some people in some areas where they would normally have an unrestricted freedom, etc. Now in a complex community, such as a State as we know it, no one can escape subjection to at least some rules other than the general rules of the community of which he is a citizen. It is only some that find this so tiresome that they go to the extent of becoming beachcombers or vagrants in order to escape the maximum possible of the rules that can be escaped.

This is certain to have a very significant influence on the development of the communal structure, for membership of bodies and sub-communities clearly will create wishes and expectations. Some of them will sooner or later come to be implemented in the rule structure of the community itself. The trade union movement is an example.

Reciprocally, the community imposes obvious limits on its sub-structures, of which enough examples were given in the above.

Bodies can be formed for the explicit purpose of effecting such changes in the social structure as for instance are temperance societies and political parties. Thus deliberate attempts at social engineering can emerge. In order to see how these can operate, a considerable amount of analysis of a different order is needed. In this book we can do no more than to indicate how this could be done.

CHAPTER VI

STRUCTURE OF BELIEFS AND GROUP STRUCTURE

Up till now the discussion in this book was confined to the logically possible. Nothing was said about likely developments, nothing about for example the type of belief, agreement or policy that is likely to arise. This was the object of the exercise, but nonetheless it might be profitable to ask some questions which are outside the strict province of the initial search.

One of these questions concerns the type of belief, expectation, wish, or desire, that can or would be likely to become the basis of: a co-operation between people; a standing arrangement; a rule; a policy, etc. This overflows into the question of a relation between a possible system of beliefs, and the social structure that might be related to it. Thus it might, for instance, be asked whether a system of rules requires a system of beliefs? If it does, would the beliefs be independent of the administrative structure, its basis, or its product, and what type of belief is likely to be significant in this connection.

These issues can be to a large extent discussed in principle in a non-empirical manner. The results are likely to be illuminating for e.g. such questions as: Are beliefs, and in particular explicit beliefs, the foundation on which a society is built? At the very least, we might be less likely to be satisfied with ostensibly plausible observations, and more inclined to investigate the less obvious but possibly more significant features of the situation.

It will be quite clear that not every belief, wish or desire lends itself to entrenchment in a co-operative arrangement, be it standing or *ad hoc*, for example: The wish that my toothache would stop; The belief that it *should* rain; Everybody's wish that no one should ever die; Mary's wish that she could keep to her diet, etc. Some wishes are quite futile, and some projects do not lend themselves to social engineering, even if not futile. The first question is then: What features must a wish[1] possess to lend itself to co-operative handling?

Firstly a wish must be a genuine *wish* to be socially potent, it must be the type of wish, or desire whose fulfilment can be envisaged in an intelligible manner. For instance: "I wish that something satisfactory would happen" said in a situation where nothing seems to work, is a description of one's state, but it does not specify a viable wish or desire of any kind. While it is possible to maintain that one has here a wish for some change to the better, it will be clear that the ideas of one who has this "wish" are so vague that it is impossible to know what will satisfy his need, he does not know this himself. In this the wish is a *pseudo-wish*, for though in a case like this we can communicate an emotional *wishing tone*, we cannot communicate *what is wanted*. For the present purpose it is best to say that to state one's wish is the same as saying what one wants and *to have a wish is to know what one wants*. Only then on the basis of a statement of a wish steps can be taken to satisfy the want, an agreement can be reached, etc. and it is the possibility of taking such steps that makes a wish socially and communally interesting. This is for the obvious reason that below this threshold no social action can be taken, since no action can be taken. Thus pseudo-wishes are socially impotent.

Secondly, and equally obviously, a socially significant wish, i.e. what could in principle be acted upon, must be *communicable*, and it is not communicable in at least two types of case:

(a) Where only a private appreciation of what one wishes to be done is possible. Suppose that John Doe had a mystical experience as the result of which he both feels enlightened, and knows the frame of mind that will produce a similar mystical trance in anybody. He might wish that everybody should put himself in such a frame of mind, and gain the "insight." But if the "insight" alone makes the request intelligible – his wish is *intrinsically incommunicable* and socially impotent.

(b) Where the means of communication are lacking. Putting aside the trivial problem of a foreigner without the knowledge of the local language, we can think of a more serious case. This might happen when someone gets an idea intrinsically communicable, but such that it is on a different wave-length from that of his peers. Thus an original member of the Franciscan order, suddenly struck with the Chinese-style need for saving face, might have found it impossible to communicate his idea to other brothers, yet the Chinese have no such difficulty.

[1] I use "wish" to stand for any applicable attitude, and will continue to do so for the sake of brevity.

In such circumstances his wish would have been *contingently incommunicable* and socially impotent.

A genuine and communicable wish could be formally excluded in any given society, i.e. it might not be permitted to state and/or implement such a wish. An example is provided by the offence of "soliciting" in terms of which a prostitute is entitled both to have and to gratify her wish to sell sexual favours, but is not permitted to state the wish.

A statement of such an excluded wish cannot properly lead to a favourable and acceptable action in the community that excludes it, but sometimes it can lead to action against the offenders i.e. those who ask and/or those who grant such a request, for it is possible for individuals to act at variance with the rules of the community. Thus in the Holy Roman Empire anti-religious and anti-god wishes were excluded and offenders were dealt with severely, but there were offenders, as there is soliciting in e.g. Australia. To qualify the above point it is necessary to observe that such wishes of offenders are not strictly speaking socially idle, even though their efficacy is thwarted whenever possible.

Thus it should be noted that exclusion is in principle different from incommunicability or lack of genuineness of a wish. An excluded wish is clearly socially possible if infelicitous. There would be no need to exclude it if it was futile in itself. In fact it must be excluded by an arrangement based on the acceptance of a wish that contradicts it, and the existence and/or acceptance of this second-order wish cannot be necessary. Consequently, if a wish is excluded, it need not stay so, and it is effectively excluded only if the communal expectation to have it excluded is treated seriously by a sufficient proportion of the members of the community in question – there must be an effective standing arrangement concerning the wish-suppression in question.

When a wish is communicable and acceptable it need not be communicated *expressis verbis* as long as it is made known to relevant parties. However the explicit expression of a wish can be made a *conditio sine qua non* of its acceptability in this, that or another case. This is usual in e.g. law, where explicit decisions must be reached by explicit procedures relating to explicit rules. In other cases insinuating wishes might do, or it might be obvious or understood that certain wishes exist. (The last in particular can be disconcerting to strangers.) One finds this kind of arrangement in some cases in Britain where it is regarded as obvious that for example parking cannot be permitted in certain streets, whereas it might be permitted in other narrower streets. Efficiency demands that wishes should not be regarded as obvious, or insinuations as binding, unless it is obvious to all concerned that this is the case. A sophisticated system will be explicit, though a less explicit system might require more sophisticated people to run it.

Even the most sophisticated society rests ultimately on the rules that form its basic structure, and it is here *par excellence* that the standing communal wishes are operative though not explicitly promulgated and stated. Habits can be easily more numerous than the number of rules that could be conceivably observed in a self-conscious explicit manner. It is not even typical for a habit to have its origin in an observance of an explicit arrangement.

Thirdly, a socially potent wish must be sufficiently *clear and definite* for its purpose. Suppose a wife says, without further explanation, "I wish that you were a better husband"; a leader of the Opposition wishes for more efficient and wiser actions on the part of the Government; a conductor wants a better standard of play by his orchestra; in each case the wish is communicable – we know what would satisfy the wishes: a better husband; more efficient actions; better standard of play. But we do not have enough information for the construction of working agreements. Contrast here a definite wish such as: "I wish you to stop snoring." On the other hand the acceptance of a general wish is compatible with an indefinite range of actions. This of course is insufficient to form the basis of a particular rule, but it might be sufficient to support a general maxim. However even maxims must amount to agreements that can be either complied with or broken, by the parties concerned. If it can never be established whether the agreement was broken or not by a given action the respective general wish is quite futile and socially sterile. Take as an example a capricious girl saying to her lover: "You should really make a better effort to try to please me." In a way we know what is wanted – he should do whatever pleases her at any given moment without asking what it was, and if he had telepathic insight he could comply. Her whims can be complied with. But in the given circumstances the information is essentially insufficient to carry out the project, thus the lady's wish is essentially ineffective.

It should be observed that even effective maxims are insufficient as the only or the foundation rules of a community for social structure must be based ultimately on clear arrangements concerning what the members of a community are to do and are not to do. Only this will provide tangible and definite limits and prescriptions, and enable individuals to place confidence in what others are likely to do, or refrain from doing. If the rule in question was so general or so framed that it would not be clear what action it demanded, and since appropriate actions would then depend on its interpretation, no one could be certain of the rule and its consequences. Such arrangements would be of little use because, as Hobbes has noticed,[2] people would still be quite uncertain as to what others are likely to do, and it is their actual actions, rather than the justifications of them, that affect communal life. It is the confidence in what others will *do* that makes inter-individual co-operation possible in the first place.

This is not to deny the obvious, namely that general rules are both possible and useful. But they are possible only against the background of co-operation based ultimately on a sufficient set of particular rules, whose effect on the behaviour of individuals is not open to serious question.

In a sophisticated community the existence of co-operation, confidence, etc. is taken for granted, and useful agreements on general policy matters are possible. Not surprisingly maxims tend to be regarded as important for they provide guidelines where ground-level arrangements offer no help.

Taking all this into account we should reiterate that a wish *which is to be socially potent must be clear enough to lend itself to adoption as a basis of an arrangement for co-operation* – basically it will be a wish that has clear implications for a definite course of action, but sometimes, in a special and dependent situation, a much less definite arrangement might be socially significant, and then a less definite wish is adequate.

In any case it must be agreed what would count as an acceptable result of a course of action adopted under the agreement. In a general and vague case such as a wish for better governmental efficiency it should be for example agreed that achieving the same results with less expenditure and less manpower is an improvement. Anyone who would deny this and claim that the crucial point of efficiency is the provision of maximum public service sinecures, could not co-operate with the rest in terms of this wish.[3] This might have clear practical implications. The type of arrangement possible in any given case will depend not only on the degree of precision and explicitness desirable from the point of view of social engineering, but also on the character of wishes, and *mutatis mutandis*, needs. If these are general only general rules are pos-

[2] T. Hobbes, *Leviathan*, Chapters 17 and 18.

[3] Though providing jobs for as many as possible could be a sound government policy in some circumstances.

sible. A wish might reach such a level of vagueness that it will not be fit even as a basis of a most general maxim, and then it becomes a mere expression of a sentiment. Thus with a pseudo-maxim: "Try to please at least some God." Without at least some elucidation, this provides no guidelines whatever.

Sometimes the vagueness of an arrangement could be due not to the nature of the wish as above, but to a failure of communication. Let us think of a case where the participants have agreed to work towards improved efficiency. Further each of the individuals has a workable idea of efficiency, as well as some idea of how to attempt to improve on the existing standard. But these ideas do not tally. In such a case what John Doe is doing might be contrary to what Richard Roe is attempting while each tries to act in accordance with the general agreement. The wish is both viable and communicable in principle, for an explanation accessible to both will remedy the situation, but unless such an explanation, or equivalent, is given the arrangement is faulty through lack of precision. The expectations of participants are likely to be thwarted through a misunderstanding. Such an arrangement need not be completely sterile in practice, for each of the participants when confronted with, say, a change in a bank procedure will know at once whether, according to him, the set-up is more or less efficient than before. In such a case the arrangement while vague at the beginning can become more explicit when the parties are confronted with *yea* and *nay* candidates in practice, and reach interpretative agreements. In this way better communication and a more satisfactory arrangement could be obtained.

Of course it is possible to attempt to reach some kind of an arrangement even with a wish that is in fact vague in the way described above. But then in reaching the arrangement a risk is taken – for it is *assumed* that all participants have the same, or very similar, ideas after all. If when the actual cases come there is little or no difference, the risk comes off, as often it does. In the opposite case the arrangement is likely to break down completely, unless it is effectively re-arranged to suit the situation, e.g. in the manner envisaged in the previous paragraph.

Basically in an actual social situation all that is required is that the individuals concerned should all get the idea definitely and precisely enough to adopt it as the basis of a workable arrangement. This includes the wish, whose wish it is, and who is to adopt it. But it is immaterial how the understanding should be reached, any method that will provide it is enough. Success is conditional on achieving *in fact* mutual understanding sufficient for practical purposes.

Fourthly, the wish must admit of social and co-operative handling in order to be socially significant in the full sense. In the first section above some futile wishes were mentioned, for example, "I wish that nobody should ever die" – these admit of no handling at all. But some wishes though not utterly futile are socially suspect for they are not open to action by social i.e. interpersonal action. Take for example the wish that I should concentrate on my work. This work is socially futile but not futile in itself. The community cannot do anything about it, but I can try and can even succeed in doing something about it. I can show determination not to try to work out my plans for a holiday while writing this text. I can resolutely put out of my mind any extraneous matter that comes into it: I can try to shut my ears to street noises, etc. But *others cannot* do any of these things *for me*. The same is true of such wishes as: wishing that I could come to decisions more readily; wishing that one should let others talk him into things he does not want to do, etc.

With these wishes it is not the case that agreements have no point at all. For it is after all possible for a number of people to agree that each will make an effort to concentrate on his work. It is also possible to try to do this, i.e. to keep or to break the agreement. But the communal point of such agreements is limited for these objects cannot be communal objects, at least not in any direct way. My concentration cannot be the direct object of communal action for it is a purely personal matter and achievement. Others can try to create favourable conditions, atmosphere, etc. for my effort but they cannot make the effort themselves. To claim that this is a typical case of communal effort is not to take the point. As suggested there can be an agreement that e.g. no one should try to distract me while I am working, or produce numerous alternatives when I am trying to decide etc. etc. But all such co-operation is aimed merely at making the job easier for me. And these actions fulfil a wish, i.e. that people should not make concentration difficult for me when I am working, etc. But this wish is not the wish that I should concentrate, and only I can act directly on this latter wish.

A social or co-operative effort *par excellence* exists where a number of individuals act on the one wish – strive for the one goal. Yet when twenty people are trying to concentrate each of them is doing something different even though all the goals are similar. John Doe tries to have John Doe concentrate, Richard Roe wishes Richard Roe to concentrate, etc. This can be socially significant: A group all of whose members concentrate will achieve more than one where only some do, but these individual efforts do not constitute concerted action, they merely contribute to the possibility of effective concerted action. Such efforts cannot provide the basic co-operation necessary to make communal life possible, but where there is communal life such secondary agreements can be not only worthwhile but important for they can have social consequences, albeit in a dependent way.

These difficulties are not limited to matters where this, that or another person has privileged access to something, i.e. to subjective, internal achievements.

Suppose I wish that I shall complete this book within twelve months. Now this is not an achievement in the subjective sphere, like controlling one's excitability would be. More than one person can write a book under the title "Elements of Social and Political Philosophy," and more than one person can contribute to the same book. Still the wish expressed is not amenable to social co-operation in any direct sense. If a team of researchers were to finish the book for me, the wish would not be fulfilled, for *I* would not have finished it – to wish or plan to do something oneself is not a social project, for example, learning to drive is not, but it can have social consequences, for example if *X* can drive *X* can offer his services as a driver to the District Nursing Service, etc. Such socially futile projects are more numerous than one might suppose, for instance, it is socially futile to try to have someone learn something, though it is not futile to try to teach him something or to make it easy and attractive for him to learn it. This leads to what might be termed indirect social action. Conditions conducive towards the desired end can be created – e.g. schools, teachers, premiums for those who learn, etc. can be established. That these methods are indirect can be concealed by the fact that often they are reasonably reliable. But their reliability is statistical – most children will learn at least this much in such and such conditions, but some will learn less, or not at all, and there is no helping this. Punitive and coercive methods, unless consisting in use of direct force to achieve a direct end, are also indirect, the desired effect is the effect of the existence of these methods, but not a direct product of them, the direct product being prison terms enforced on criminals, etc. This makes them unfit as the basic foundation of communal structure.

There are projects that seem in a very good sense inter-personal, that can be dealt with in some ways, but do not lend themselves to social engineering. The obvious example here is private morality. If one were to distinguish between being an immoral person and doing things to others that are not morally acceptable, one could sketch the demarcation line as follows: Other-regarding social actions that are morally unacceptable are typically, though perhaps not exclusively, those making people miserable or unhappy. Immoral actions that do not affect others would include: corrupting oneself; having ill thoughts; taking delight in the suffering of others (as distinct from contributing to such suffering); wishing people ill; etc. Being thoroughly immoral on the second count is completely compatible with never *acting* in a morally reprehensible way in the social other-regarding context.

Clearly we can have rules, agreements, etc., to prevent people suffering from the immoral action of others, but we cannot have any co-operative method that would make any impression on the other type of immorality. In a sense things like ill-will, etc. are the concern of others, not only of the ill-minded, but they cannot be handled by others. If we were to designate the doing of things to others, or doing of things that can affect others as public, and all other morally significant doings even concerned with others, as private morality, we should say that any wish concerned with private morality was socially sterile – it cannot be effectively handled by corporate effort. We can make people conform, and we can prevent them from making a nuisance of themselves, but we cannot make them better – socially we must be satisfied if they are better behaved. This is in fact very obvious. An individual of sadistic disposition who seeks out and enjoys watching people in pain and distress, e.g. accident victims, is not a very pleasant character. If through fear of reprisals he refrains from contributing to, and/or producing such distress, he is socially very much more acceptable than if he did. But internally he is just as unpleasant in both cases.

If the society were to prevent the passive sadist from indulging his harmless pleasures it would be unlikely to make him better. In fact deprived and frustrated he could easily become worse. If he manages to satisfy himself at no cost to others e.g. by reading Marquis de Sade, the society is not a loser, and if this is prevented neither he nor society gain anything. Thus social action is here obviously futile.

A socially potent wish can form a basis of a co-operative agreement either *ad hoc* or *standing*, in the latter case of course it must be a standing wish or a standing expectation.

Nothing more need be said if the investigation is limited to single arrangements, rules, etc. That they form clusters will be obvious, but since single wishes, as much as single rules can support, limit or contradict each other, the relations between the expectations are as easily understood as relations between the rules and arrangements.

With respect to a code, or a system of codes, a number of further questions will arise. A code was defined as a set of rules that controls, in a systematic way, an area of activity, over which it is understood to have authority. This set of rules must be structured for the rules implement jointly a policy. It is conceivable that such a policy could be completely accidental, a simple mean-result of independently conceived rules, which however are understood to belong to the only cluster consisting of all rules that have authority in the area. This unlikely case can be safely left aside.

To use a language that implies more explicit engineering than need be the case: the set of rules forming a code is usually "calculated" to have a joint effect, the rules are "designed" with each other and the general policy in view. Thus the rules are related systematically, but since they are just arrangements implementing expectations and wishes, the wishes, expectations, etc., that form the basis of these rules must also be systematically related to each other, forming a *system of expectations*. What is the inter-relation between a system of expectations and a corresponding system of rules? Is a system of expectations needed before the system of rules, can both arise together, could the system of rules come to exist first?

(1) Clearly it is possible to *create a system of rules to implement a system of wishes or beliefs that we already have*. For if there is a system of beliefs to the effect that for example freedom and safety are both important and that if all of us were to do *a. b. c. d. e. . . . n.* in appropriate circumstances freedom would be enhanced without any detriment to safety, and if we were to do –, –, –, –, . . . –, in appropriate circumstances, safety would be enhanced without detriment to freedom. We might make an arrangement with respect to each of these actions, creating a system of rules amounting to a "freedom with safety" code.

Our beliefs would then turn into expectations, for by then we not only believe that x will enhance safety without detriment to freedom, and believe that therefore it would be advisable if people did x, but also expect them to x in appropriate circumstances. Similarly with all the other relevant particular wishes.

(2) *The other way is also possible.* Here the process could start with the establishment of some rules thought of as separate. But these rules

would be likely to affect each other. For example, an absolute rule of priority of women over men and an absolute rule of priority of U-people over non-U-people will not work together if some non-U-people are women. Such problems are likely to arise on very many points, necessitating dovetailing of procedures, not only at the point of conflict, but at many others. For a change in one place might and often will create a new situation somewhere else. The U/non-U priority rule will be in accord with servant master-type rules if masters are U and servants are non-U, for then the rules support each other. But since a master who cannot command is not a master, a non-U sergeant must take priority over a U-recruit, the same with impoverished aristocratic chauffeurs working for nouveau-riche plebeian millionaires. If such situations arise the U-preference rule must be either abandoned or amended.

These problems would tend to lead to a formation of a cluster of rules. Given this, some rules and/or sets of rules cannot be had comfortably in a given cluster, others can. It would be reasonable to select rules and/or sets that (a) are comfortable, that is, do not lead to strife, and (b) accomplish as many of the agreed common aims as possible. But to do this is to think systematically about the area of behaviour for now rules are seen as parts of a *system of control*. Accordingly the relevant expectations and the corresponding wishes in the area will form a system. But this system of beliefs *arose out of problems of social administration* and answers the need for comfortable and strifeless social and communal structure.

Thus: (a) it is not necessary for group structure to reflect any preexisting *systematic set* of beliefs as such for it can form independently from an already existing belief structure. It can do this by interplay of rules embodied in co-operative arrangements, but it must be observed that each such arrangement presupposes at least one prior belief on which a wish is based. (b) For practical reasons social expectations must be to a large extent systematic, otherwise the arrangements based on them would tend to become unmanageable. That such a system of beliefs can come to be regarded as mores or morals is another matter, and another possible development. Significantly arrangements quite preposterous on other grounds could work together easily. For instance given a rule that subjects done as single subjects in the University are not to count for a degree, and a rule that no other philosophy subjects can be taken unless Philosophy I is taken first, then it is feasible, though not reasonable, to require anyone who passed Philosophy I as a single subject, to repeat it if he wishes to do any further philosophy subject for his degree. Such was in fact the administrative advice given to some students.

The *consistency requirement* is thus relatively content-independent; all that is required is that rules in a system supplement, support or permit each other, and that they should not contradict, contravene or nullify each other. We could call this requirement a formal requirement.

Clearly not every consistent and formally feasible system of rules is desirable, for a consistent system could promote heartbreak and unhappiness with a single-minded dedication. Naturally enough, it would be foolish to observe a code of behaviour if on every point such an observance would be detrimental to oneself and others. But things are never as simple as that.

Everyone expects some good to come from his relations with others, either singly or in a group. The possible goods can be divided into two classes: the *satisfaction of needs* and the *implementation of convictions*. This is a basic distinction, and naturally rough for finer distinctions could be drawn and on top of this needs and convictions interact, can create each other and sometimes can hardly be distinguishable from one another. It is best for the present moment to concentrate on needs, for needs are more tangible than demands and convictions, and naturally form the basis of both.[4]

The reference to needs might seem to introduce normative ideas, and indeed is tied to the concept of a good system. But it is not intended to refer here to what is worthy of approval in a moral or ideological sense. The basic satisfactoriness of a communal system is to be tied to organic or natural needs of the individuals. Thus one might approve of Japanese bonsai gardens and dislike fully grown trees, but see that a miniature tree was deprived of the satisfaction of some of its needs.

The distinction between essential, and inessential needs should be understood similarly. An *essential need* is to be understood to be a *conditio sine qua non* of survival. Non-essential needs might be important enough but unlike essential needs even in stringent cases they can remain unsatisfied for relatively long periods of time. Among the inessential needs some will be more important than others – we can call a need *basic* if it is a condition of non-retarded growth and development and *marginal* if it does no more than provide an individual or a group satisfaction, but such that no lasting or long-term effects result if it is left unattended to.

[4] Some further treatment of convictions will be found in Chapter VII, e.g. *vide* p. 148.

This set of distinctions is neither hard nor fast, the distinction between basic and marginal needs being particularly vulnerable. Nonetheless even this provides a guide and a useful *prima facie* way of systematising the picture. It might be a guide to the usage to say that it is not safe to opt out of the satisfaction of essential needs, and not reasonable to abandon the satisfaction of basic ones, but marginal needs can be neglected. It might be unpleasant to live without music, and unsatisfactory to live without medical attention, but it is impossible to live without food and water.

To obtain simple and transparent terminology we can draw up the following table:

Type of social achievement			Type of need
Satisfaction of needs	Objective needs	ESSENTIAL	Essential needs: (*conditio sine qua non* of survival)
			Basic needs: (*conditio sine qua non* of unimpaired health and growth)
Conferring of benefits		INESSENTIAL	Marginal needs: (desirable to various degrees but can be left unsatisfied without serious consequences)
Implementation of convictions	Subjective	CONVICTIONS	Beliefs concerning needs of different kinds as well as what should be done for various possible other reasons (e.g. moral, religious, ideological, etc.)[5]

It should be remembered that those interact, e.g. a conviction can create a need and *vice versa*, and that the distinctions are open textured – it could be, for instance, essential to have some proportion of basic needs satisfied, and basic to have some marginal need and convictions satisfied, etc.

Given these qualifications at least the main distinctions between essential and inessential needs and convictions are easy enough to operate. However problems of demarcation can arise very easily. Since the classification is tied to practical and empirical problems of survival and growth, these cannot be decided on paradigmatic grounds. Here the

[5] Cf. here Chapter VII, p. 148 ff.

discussion must be limited to general points depending for their validity on the connection between e.g. essential needs and survival rather than on the detailed demarcation between e.g. non-retarded development and good life.[6] A further reason against attempting more than a general account of these distinctions can be found in this, that in different circumstances it might be necessary to assess similar requirements differently, e.g. what is basic in present-day Europe might have been marginal in Ghengis Khan's Asia, good examples might be provided by the need to learn to read and write, or the need to have at least some money, should the need be a need for a reasonable bank balance, this would not be intelligible in tribal conditions, and yet it could be near to essential in some possible societies.

Secondly we can talk of the *needs of an individual* and the *needs of a community*. Significantly what is essential for a community might not be essential for the individual. Thus the existence of co-operative arrangements is strictly necessary for a community, but an individual can exist without it albeit uncomfortably. If it were a necessary condition of his unretarded development to live communally, he would have a basic need for both community and a fortiori for co-operation – which is the idea expressed by saying that man is a political animal.[7]

It might appear obvious that in any given community needs would be taken care of in order of importance. Essential first and then Basic and Marginal in reverse order of dispensability. But this is an obvious over-simplification for: (a) a choice might exist between wishes of similar weight; (b) people can be mistaken about the relative importance of needs; and (c) people can fail to act reasonably.

Some of the wishes capable of social realisation are more likely to be implemented than others. Certain conditions responsible for this can be discerned on very general grounds.

Thus the prospect must recommend itself to those who are about to agree to co-operate with one another, or else the agreement is likely to founder.[8] It seems obvious that a proposal will not recommend itself to one if it does not seem to fulfil any of his needs but it appears sure to thwart some of them. But an arrangement could easily be adopted by those who expect that as the result of this their need-satisfaction

[6] Which is of course the point of the next distinction.

[7] Cf. here: Aristotle, *Politica*, Book I, Ch. 2. Aquinas, *De Regimine Principum*, Book I, Ch. I, par. 4, 5.

[8] Clearly the individuals concerned need not have any explicit awareness that x recommends itself but y does not, as long as they react to them as if they did, thus if we have a need an explicit and articulate demand is not always necessary.

will be increased, consequently it may not be as simple to determine where the balance lies, as it might seem. Let a *subjective need* be the requirement for that which an individual *sees* as needed to promote his well-being, quite independently of the correctness of the belief in question, an *objective need* that which will *in fact* promote his well-being, quite independently of his beliefs.[9]

Clearly subjective needs are more likely to move people to action than objective, but unknown needs. Thus an objective need i.e. something that will enable an individual to: survive, or develop, or live comfortably, might not lead to action if the relevant facts are not known. So for instance, a need for medical attention if not realised by the patient would be unlikely to move him to action. At the same time the desire for protection from ghosts, a subjective and spurious need, may lead to urgent action. If people were motivated by the objective state of affairs rather than by their appreciation of it, both propaganda and advertising would be out of place. How then is it possible to determine what moves people to co-operate in certain ways? It is impossible to rely on the objective situation, but to disregard the objective need position would be misleading as well. The question is complicated further by the fact that some needs while felt, are not articulate and do not lead to felt convictions. This is certainly a matter for empirical investigation, but not easy or direct for people can often fail to be explicitly aware of the reasons that led them to adopt this or that arrangement, and indeed even of the existence of the arrangement itself. To guess at the reasons on the basis of the observation of existing arrangements would seem unwise. At any rate, such an investigation would be clearly beyond the scope of the present book.

Thus if the above criterion were expected to provide the explanation in actual cases where co-operative arrangements exist, it would be useless. But it can be used to indicate what kind of arrangement is likely to be implemented, and might help in discovering law-like relationships. We can safely say that if an arrangement is obviously disadvantageous to all concerned it is unlikely to succeed, and if it does an explanation is necessary. If it is obviously advantageous the opposite is the case. From this certain conclusions about communal structure can be drawn. Thus a normal society will adopt a majority of arrangements that make life easier and simplify the problems of living with other men. An arrangement appearing to participants to be obviously ad-

[9] This makes it possible for Rousseau to talk of us being *forced to be free*. Cf. *The Social Contract*. Cf. also Hegel.

vantageous to all concerned alike is likely to be adopted.[10] If an arrangement exists it is likely that it: is, was, appears, or appeared to be advantageous to most concerned. People do not rush happily into accepting agreements clearly detrimental to their well-being and *vice versa*. In political practice terror is often used to make acceptance of certain otherwise unattractive arrangements advantageous.

General observation supports this conclusion. In any community annoying and detrimental interference with other individuals is outlawed to a very large degree. In fact it is hard to realise the full extent of this. A consideration of wilful children might help. They kick each other, take each other's toys away only to throw them aside, maliciously spoil each other's fun, scratch, pull, annoy each other, etc. Most of their actions seem both pointless and annoying, but then the annoyance seems to be the point of the performance. Even a malicious anarchist does not act in this way, for clearly he accepts the basic social limits. Now to see the strength of the need-satisfaction principle it is only necessary to envisage a community where, compared with such children, as much additional annoyance is made compulsory as is outlawed in ours. It is quite clear that such an arrangement will not exist in practice. What sort of fools would people have to be to go to the length of trying to organize themselves in this way?

To give a particular example, suppose that a communal rule states that a man awake should not ever let another fall asleep. The citizens would be unlikely to develop pro-attitudes to this way of life. But suppose *per impossibile* that they stay with it, and further accept more of equally uncomfortable and possibly dangerous arrangements. Very soon a point must come where not only the citizens will be completely disillusioned, but where survival will become extremely difficult. While it is possible to describe a sophisticated system of arrangements implementing a mischievously malicious policy, in practice the individuals attempting to live it would soon be unfit to do anything much, weakened as they would be by e.g. the lack of sleep, the need to avoid others when doing anything at all (think of duties of food spilling, tripping, and other possible obstructionist rules, etc.). Thus the system would be self-defeating in two ways: (a) It would render the presence of others an uncomfortable impediment and so render most reasonable a desire for solitude, and (b) it would prevent anything useful from being

[10] Cf. here K. Marx, *A Contribution to the Critique of Political Economy*, Preface. Marx takes economic factors to be both dominant and the only ones capable of "scientific" treatment, i.e. capable of objective and accurate assessment – it will be reasonably obvious that both claims are exaggerated.

achieved by communal effort. It is not merely better but *necessary* that the arrangement should be *advantageous on the whole*, which is not to say that things could not be largely or comparatively uncomfortable, e.g. since people react to what they believe, rather than reacting to what is the case, an arrangement objectively uncomfortable could arise if the participants thought it advantageous. In some circumstances a system of human sacrifice with victims chosen by lot, could be adopted for instance if it was thought necessary in order to avoid the terrible wrath of the gods, yet it is clear that such a system puts every citizen at a very considerable disadvantage. But this sort of thing is most likely to happen on a reasonably sophisticated level. For unreasonable and explicit beliefs are characteristically the result of intercourse between people, and that requires language and many other things. But the really basic co-operative arrangements are more primitive than explicit communication arrangements, and can not be conditioned by them.

Significantly the really basic co-operative arrangements are more primitive than explicit communication arrangements since they are presupposed by them. What is more this basic organization is presupposed in any sophisticated arrangement, and that includes all explicit co-operation, which clearly is relatively very sophisticated since it implies *inter alia* the possession of a practically useful, even if not necessarily articulate concept of co-operative arrangement. Now since systems of beliefs must be explicit in order to be deliberately embodied in communal structure, the first systematisation must come the other way round – from the needs of co-operation, as evidenced in inter-personal practice, for these can be as simple and unsophisticated as need be.

To this it might be objected that needs might be determined by beliefs, and that for example, morals, though possibly systematic from an outsider's point of view, need not be a matter of the holding of explicit general beliefs linked into a systematic whole of which one is aware as such. There is some force in this objection, even though it creates a lot of unfortunate confusion.

It is true that not only human, but also animals' reactions to their environment are largely systematic. Chickens attempt to eat grain, bathe in water, avoid dogs and fires, etc. And chickens are not very intelligent. They are not capable of any kind of articulate thought or belief.

A *systematic reaction to the world*, for example the form one's reactions in different cases do and might take, should be distinguished from a *system of articulate beliefs* (and/or practices), that is, the holding of explicit views systematically connected to each other, concerning for example, action. A systematic reaction can be moral, if the individuals concerned have moral sense just as it can be kind if they are kind. But this is not the same as the holding of moral beliefs, these must in the nature of the case be articulate *viz.* at least statable in principle.

It is clear that unless individuals reacted systematically no co-operation could ever arise, for any arrangement presupposes the ability to act in a systematically repetitious way – in fact any practice does. Since a practice must be systematically repetitious there must be some criterion of correct performance.[11] This can be found in the reaction of individuals to each other. If the action is correct others acquiesce, if it is not they react negatively. For this explicit holding of beliefs is not needed. It will be sufficient if the systematic reaction of other individuals is *de facto* a test of the reaction of any one of them. In fact the possibility of this very primitive type of check is a precondition for the formation of language. It is only when language arises that explicit and articulate arrangements can be made, yet co-operation is possible on a basis simpler than that.

But this does not involve the holding of articulate beliefs. To hold an articulate belief is to not only react in a systematic manner but also to think that one must or should do so. If one knows that one is or could be acting, one knows that one has a choice, and also that in similar circumstances a similar range of choices is likely to present itself. It is only then that one can hold the view that a certain action is appropriate or obligatory in certain circumstances. Clearly then in the basic case the emergence of communal structure must be independent of the people subscribing to a prior system of articulate beliefs. For it is the existence of the basic arrangements, e.g. as to use of words, that alone makes it possible to form articulate beliefs.

No community can be ultimately and originally based on a system of beliefs held prior to its existence by its prospective members, and commence with a systematic implementation of those. But people who have learned to form, and have formed, such explicit belief in communities *a*, *b*, *c*, . . . *n*, could band together and set out explicitly to form a new community – starting from belief implementation. This however is a development parasitic on the normal one, and furthermore it cannot cover all basic sub-structure rules of the new community, as will become clear in subsequent discussion.

[11] Cf. L. Wittgenstein, *Philosophical Investigations*, Sections 258 ff.

It is not the case that in every type of development a system of beliefs is secondary to a system of rules. This can be seen clearly on the example of a pragmatic but sophisticated situation such as creation of an air traffic code. This could never happen, at least not in the form it has now, unless people: (a) saw the need for a code; (b) had an idea what contingencies it should cover; (c) knew what was to be avoided, etc. Thus here the existence of a practical code presupposes that people hold certain beliefs. Thus both the ways are possible – a system of beliefs can lead to a system of arrangement and *vice versa*.

It might be claimed that in very primitive situations either beliefs and co-operative arrangements both arise at the same time or neither do. This is plausible provided only that: attitudes, implicit beliefs, etc. are admitted as beliefs, for if they are not, grave problems will arise with respect to implicit non-articulate rules, habits and the like. In the above discussion I have, for clarity's sake, used "belief" to exclude these less articulate elements, and in this terminology the ground level co-operative arrangements are primary with respect to beliefs i.e. articulate wishes and/or attitudes. A wish or attitude can be articulate only if it is not totally implicit. Where only implicit elements are to hand beliefs are as yet out of place.

It is possible to discern implicit and explicit communal arrangements. *The first* govern actions that are typically done automatically, where doing otherwise is simply unthinkable, for instance we do not spit in the faces of passers-by, nor do we pour acid on the clothes of strangers, etc. Where *the second* is concerned we typically do something because we *know* that we should, we are also in a better position to object to the arrangement in question.

I shall call a set of implicit arrangements, such that they determine the style of interpersonal behaviour on a certain level in a given group – the *basic communal structure*. I shall call the set of mainly explicit rules (or arrangements) such that it determines the further interpersonal relation of its members *the superstructure of the community*.

Much of the communal co-operation is grounded in implicit rules of behaviour, dovetailed together in that the object of all of them is to make living and living in company bearable and/or pleasant in very obvious ways. It is not surprising that this basic structure is not easily amenable to direct handling. To handle these arrangements we first of all have to become explicitly aware of their existence and nature, and this is not always an easy matter. Secondly we would have to set out to change them, that is, to move from the stage where the basic rules $a, b, c, d, \ldots,$

n are generally accepted, *viz.* expectation , , , , . . . are regarded as reasons for acting in ways A, B, C, D, . . . N, to the stage where they are not, where some or all of them are replaced by others. But naturally at this level there are no obvious techniques for doing this. These rules were not promulgated, consequently no one can be an authority entitled to handle them. It would seem that the only method would consist in changing directly people's acceptance of these expectations, for if a sufficient number of individuals abandoned them, the rules in question would lapse. But how is this mass change of heart to be achieved? Clearly this is almost an impossible job. In fact basic rules *can* and generally do change gradually as people's attitudes alter. But mostly the process goes on unnoticed and is visible clearly only in historical perspective. An individual might try to act in such a way as to enhance the change of attitudes in a certain direction, e.g. he can break the customs, argue about them, write plays or novels, etc., in the hope of affecting the attitudes of others. Such action might have some effect but even at best one cannot hope for dramatic results. In this way the basic communal structure is solidly ponderous, and this is, for obvious reasons, almost entirely to the good.

It is possible of course, if the machinery is at hand, to promulgate an explicit law directly contrary to an existing basic communal rule. But (a) it is a risky business likely to produce more strife than any but a very important matter would warrant, and (b) it can be used only in a limited fashion, that is, only very few of such basic rules can be counteracted at any given time.

Now to comment on these points.

Ad (a): Let us think of an example. We promulgate a law stating that in a public situation everybody is obliged to refuse to do what any other person might ask him to do, and that requests might be granted where there are no more than two persons present, but in no other circumstances.

What we contradict here is not the most basic of rules, but it is intuitively clear and thus a good example. Now people are not permitted to do the hitherto obvious and consider a request on its merits alone. The consequences of such a rule would be drastic –e.g. a banquet at which one could not for example ask for sugar unless one got the hostess off to a private room beforehand, but how would one do that? If you think this is too tough, limits requesting by an age formula, sex formula, age and sex formula, or occupation formula of some sort; for example: requests can be granted only by an older member of the same sex; to a junior member of the opposite sex; to a child not of age; by an official in an exercise of his duty; or when only the two people are present. People brought up according to this set of rules could work them, possibly even work them smoothly – pairs would disappear in dark corners for many more purposes than they do nowadays, and there would be a lot of subtle requesting and position jockeying going on – the art of politics would be much more skilled. If this seems odd, let us remember that some of our taboos might appear no less ridiculous to a complete stranger.

But practically speaking to one who did not have this in his blood the situation would be quite bewildering and unmanageable. We can see homely examples of a similar kind with respect to social graces, or if you wish, diplomatic protocol, or cases of those who find themselves exposed to unfamiliar taboo and politeness systems. It is not only that one does not like the new situation, one has the gravest difficulty in trying to cope with it, even if one carries with him at all times a book of etiquette rules, it might be difficult to find the right rule even if one remembered to consult the handbook.

Thus to introduce something directly opposed to a basic communal rule leads to very obvious inconvenience, and since convenience in dealing with problems to which such rules are relevant was the point of having them (more likely than not), it is quite a price to pay. But a greater good might be thus achieved. In a society where it is a matter of, say, religious belief that all proper requests should be granted, it might be necessary to make it much more difficult to present a proper request. It might work for something like Australian aborigines who have to share what they possess with any tribal member who asks for a share. It might be easier to make asking difficult than to change people's minds about granting proper requests, for they might accept easily all sorts of new taboos. But in such a case our technique would be supported by another section of our basic communal rules and this is a significant element of the example.

Let us also pay some attention to the fact that basic communal rules are characteristic in that they are implicit, actions in contravention of them simply appear unthinkable, dastardly, etc. Thus contravention of them is likely to arouse a great deal of feeling. People treated in this way and/or forced to act in this fashion are likely to feel degraded, threatened and uncomfortable, they are likely to resist, sabotage and disobey such uncongenial directives.

To illustrate, let us think of the not infrequent and almost always disastrous attempts to change the landed peasants' way of life and production, usually made in the name of this or that political or scientific ideology. It is at least arguable that rural communities (or sub-communities) are ground-level, and their structure there is a firm emphasis on the elements of the basic structure. If accepted such an assessment would afford a large share of the explanation of the reformer's difficulties. This suggestion is strengthened when we observe that rural communities are characterised by almost automatic conservatism, a hallmark of implicit acceptance of a way of life, and are better able than most to survive as separate units, as would be expected if a relatively small proportion of their working arrangements depended on the predominantly explicit rules imposed by their association with the ultimate communal system of which they are elements.

Ad (b): Now it is quite clear that firstly, no quick change in basic communal structure is possible without direct legislation, and secondly that such direct legislation could be only very limited. It could affect the basic rules at one point or another, but it could not seriously affect the character of the set-up as such.

The problem is simply this. We have seen the difficulties in trying to live in accordance with some unfamiliar principles in place of familiar basic rules, but we saw it in a reasonably narrow area. We did not even consider the obvious ramifications of our one proposed change. Consider them now, and suppose that a large number or even a majority of the basic rules are involved in a single change. All alterations are, to make it easier, explicitly promulgated.

Who could remember them all? Trying to live in this situation would be akin to everybody in a country, say English-speaking, being given a dictionary and a grammar-syntax book of another language, say classical Latin, and then they should be required to communicate exclusively in the new tongue – not a feasible project.

Thus even if you were to smash a community by some means, when the people who formed it re-convene as a group, they will naturally use their old language, and equally naturally they will fall back on their old communal habits; what else could they do?[12]

Living among strangers, it is possible to pick up their ways. It is a

[12] The inertia of communal structure is thus far greater than even Marx suggested. Cf. here *The Eighteenth Brumaire of Louis Bonaparte*, and 1871, Letter to Kugelman in *K. Marx and F. Engels Selected Correspondence*, p. 318, Foreign Language Publishing House, Moscow.

process always difficult and often painful, but it can be done. But it seems almost impossible to change radically and quickly the basic forms of communal intercourse as a community project, if the changes are even mildly extensive. We cannot form so many interconnected expectations on order, and explicitly. Any such explicit change must be based on something that makes the carrying out of this project feasible – but where the *basic communal structure* is concerned such support cannot be had. *It* is the ultimate support for any sort of communal project, but of course partial changes may be, and often are, attempted with varying degrees of success. This is often concealed, for the *superstructure* can alter dramatically or crumble and be replaced in a reasonably short time, and it is the superstructure that is visible. When we think of our style of life we generally think of explicit ways, means and habits. Tourists notice only very obvious explicit facets, but it is a matter of time and sensitivy to become aware of the style of the basic arrangements, we often miss them even as we are adapting to them.[13]

[13] *Vide* here adult migrants making a new life in a strange country.

CHAPTER VII

SOCIAL ENGINEERING: LEGISLATIVE SYSTEMS

Let us now turn our attention towards convictions, as distinct from simple needs. The distinction between the two is blurred, because the needs, as socially potent, are often not real needs, but needs as felt, that is, what is regarded or accepted as a need i.e. we tend to act on subjective convictions rather than objective needs.[1]

I use the term "conviction" to apply to any belief that something is: desirable, necessary, undesirable, etc., provided only that the belief is both *explicit and articulate*. This use is slightly wider than the common usage would have it, for it makes no reference whatever to the strength or fervour with which such beliefs are held. We will be interested exclusively in social convictions, namely those that concern social arrangements, social goods, goods that should, are, or could be, socially procured, etc.

Since there is no hard and fast line between beliefs that are explicit and articulate and those that are not, our distinction between what is merely felt or accepted as a need (or a peril), and a social conviction, suffers from similar vagueness. But this is not detrimental to our purpose since the great majority of cases is clear-cut one way or another. At any rate it is the principle rather than its application that we are interested in. Practical difficulties do not render a principle less important for understanding the type of case we have in mind.

The importance of the distinction lies in this, that what is explicit and articulate is amenable to direct action, or at the very least, to direct appraisal and criticism, in a way in which that which is merely understood and explicit is not. I shall not discuss separately what merely happens to be implicit, since it is not articulated, but can be articulated on demand. Any problems created by this complication are solved easily by simple application of common sense. It is, of course, salutary that implicit arrangements tend to become explicit and articulated if they

[1] Cf. the table on p. 137.

are found troublesome and inconvenient; such are the inbuilt forces of progress, and safety.

To reiterate – an objective need is roughly what has to be satisfied on the pain of creating an actual lack, a belief is not thus directly related to reality. The distinction is easily blurred, because where needs are explicitly potent they are often not potent *qua* objective, but in so far as they are what is regarded or accepted as needs, and thus their efficacy is conviction bound.

It might be reasonable to add here that objective needs have in a way a superior position *vis-à-vis* implementation for two reasons: *firstly*, if they are catered for real satisfaction results and the arrangement is thus more likely to stay. *Secondly*, if unsatisfied discomfort is likely to result with its corresponding desire for alleviation. Even if originally misguided the resulting demands tend in time to make the satisfaction of the real need more likely, for they will be effective only to the extent to which they are correct. Clearly to cater for a mistaken demand is unlikely to produce long-term satisfaction. At the same time unsatisfied objective needs, especially urgent ones, have a tendency to demand attention and thus are likely to be heard sooner or later.

Let us observe that significantly it is possible to have a conviction, even a correct conviction, e.g. a belief that it would be desirable for all to have annual dental check-ups, without the wish that communal provision to secure such an end should be made. A conviction is thus socially potent if, and only if, it creates a *demand*. Convictions and demands might but need not concern real needs, in fact a demand could be contrary to a real need or needs, *viz.* the actually voiced demand for free marketing of dangerous drugs.

Take a communal situation where a number of different convictions in a number of different fields are socially implemented in a number of respective explicit and articulate regulations. The individuals are then *aware* that such and such a regulation puts into effect such and such a conviction, etc. Along with this they must *realize* that a change in regulations (codes, systems) will implement something different and possibly: fail to support some convictions now catered for, achieve similar effects in a different way, etc.

We have noticed above that any sophisticated regulation structure needs status differences – individuals must have specialised jobs with respect to the given or code system, much in the same way in which regulations and certain sections of regulations (or sub-codes) have specialised jobs within the code, codes within the system, etc. Thus some people are leaders, or artificers or judges; some regulations deal with emergencies, contraventions, or differences of interpretation, etc. These are usually explicit, articulate, and responsive to articulately conceived needs. But there is a particualr type of second order need that people who are articulate about their social and communal arrangements must sooner or later see explicitly.

Arrangements are seldom perfect, conditions seldom unchanging. Now and then it might be necessary to adapt, change or improve this, that, or another element of the communal structure either to correct a past mistake or to cater for changing conditions or changing needs.

We have noticed above that due to their very nature, implicit rules change slowly and insensibly; one hopes that the changes are for the best, and is sometimes disappointed. They seldom change quickly, thus old-fashioned people are likely to be out of step even more than merely conventional ones. If conditions change quickly, this type of rule and more specially its capacity for adaptation is likely to be found wanting. Fortunately when conditions are fluid, hitherto implicit rules tend to become explicit, visible as conditions of discomfort, where previously they went unnoticed while lending support. Coming to notice they can be subsequently handled, *viz.* amended, replaced or abandoned.

Where the implicit arrangements are concerned new ways develop slowly and insensibly as communal expectations are shared by progressively fewer citizens, where those who disclaim them disobey the respective rules, where those who disbelieve them fail to be outraged by such behaviour, till at least a new expectation, or set of expectations, emerges as the one communally shared, and gives rise to a new arrangement (or lack of one) to replace the old.

Where the rules are articulate it is possible to do better. What is more an implicit evolutionary change would generally tend to be out of step with such open rules. It is true that even laws can become defunct long before they are repealed, *vide* the red flag law, but then to that extent the system loses its explicit and articulate character. This is highlighted if we ask: What happens if someone should appeal to an obsolescent regulation? Should he be told that this is one of the prescriptions that no one takes seriously? The question then arises, which rules should be taken seriously? It admits of no easy answer, and some of the advantages of the articulate code are lost.

Thus it is desirable that explicit rules should be explicitly amended, or repealed if a change is necessary. But for this we need an articulate procedure, that is, a code, or a system dealing with and providing for:

establishing, changing, repealing of regulations, establishing of policies, etc. It must be possible to decide: what to change; when to change it; how to change it; what policy to implement; etc.

To envisage a simple case. In a small community all explicit changes could be reached by public discussion and, say, voting in a general assembly of all citizens. However simple, this is a machinery of the required kind, but such a system has obvious limitations:

(i) In a populous community an assembly would be hard to organize if it was to be at all representative.

(ii) Where there is a sophisticated rule structure there are many rules and codes on many levels so the need for adjustment might become so frequent that calling up a general meeting to deal with it becomes quite impracticable. What is more, some regulations might become so specialised that expertise might be necessary to reach any opinion as to their suitability and effectiveness. Thus a *general* gathering of all, while cumbersome, might be technically unfit to deal with many a matter at hand.

Not surprisingly the usual machinery for social engineering is more sophisticated and more specialised than the Athenian system of a vote by all citizens gathered in the market place.

Special procedures will usually be evolved to deal with specific areas and types of problems. These will be explicit and formalised. Both the features are necessary: *Explicit,* for explicit arrangements must be explicitly modified; *Formalised,* for explicit communal arrangements are formal in that most of the rules involved are formally designed as binding. Thus to change them will require as formal an authority as the one that is keeping the rules in force.[2] Clearly not everyone, for any reason, and in any way, can order a change of arrangements. If this were the case the rules would not be binding, as anyone could bend them to his own convenience and thus escape not only compulsion but all need for compliance with the arrangements. Furthermore a change occurs if, and only if, it occurs. At one stage members of the community abide by rule R_1 at the other they replace it by rule R_{1a}. To do so they must (a) be informed of the change and its timing, (b) they must accept it, and the timing: (a) is a technical requirement – the change must be promulgated, that is, all relevant information must

[2] As will be remembered, one difficulty in changing implicit basic rules lies in that no authority proclaims them, or can modify them, they simply appear authoritative in themselves. It is *not done* to break them.

be made public, (b) is a formal requirement – the promulgation must be authoritative – there must be a sufficient reason for its acceptance. If a private citizen were to promulgate a change in the Australian divorce law it would be impotent even if all knew of it. If the parliament passed a law incorporating a change in it, but kept this fact jealously to itself, the legislation would be quite impotent.

As will be seen from the above it is necessary to have an appropriate authority to carry out the changes. Thus Councils can pass by-laws in certain areas, and Customs, Army. and other authorities might have the right to establish, change, or modify certain rules. If so, they have what is, in the widest sense of the word, a measure of legislative authority.

Take as an example the Roman office of a dictator, appointed to conduct a war. He had the authority to make, and remake any rules during the war. In contradistinction it is quite possible to set up an authority to pass only traffic regulations. These considerations introduce a new kind of problem, for now that rules are (i) explicit and (ii) can be introduced rather than grow gradually, an account is needed that will provide assurance on two points – that a rule is *effectively introduced* and *really accepted* – for this a correct procedure and a responsible authority must be established. A specialised type of arrangement and a new level of structural sophistication are thus seen to arise. It is still the case that the communal structure is ultimately based on the common acceptance of a number of rules, an acceptance that is not derived from any authority. But a method is in existence by which acceptance of rules of certain kinds can be ensured and therefore the structure itself has in some respects become an object of direct action. Communal engineering is now possible. This has obvious advantages – the system can be changed and adapted as soon as the need for it becomes apparent – it is thus in those respects less ponderous and more flexible. Now it has a better hope of remaining satisfactory in changing conditions. With all this the basic structure that *inter alia* gives rise to all the necessary authority and establishes the initial change procedures, remains stable and ponderous. A system on the whole to the good, since it prevents hasty and ill-conceived alterations taking too deep a root in the community.[3]

The existence of explicit methods providing for flexibility is a *conditio sine qua non* of a satisfactory communal system for obvious reasons. But it must be combined with stability which demands that all the

[3] *Vide* p. 149 f.

important rules, codes, etc. in the arrangement form a single system. For even if we start with a system of perfectly dovetailed regulations, etc. should we permit the introduction of separate unrelated changes in different areas, we would almost inevitably end with a motley combination of ill-assorted arrangements. In order to avoid this, any change that is introduced in a system, should be calculated to enhance or at least not to spoil, the coherence of the whole. Each separate authority might *have this in mind* when introducing new arrangements but even at best this is not sufficient. In order to ensure systematic co-operation a formal assurance of the continuance of the coherence of the system is necessary. For otherwise this essential feature could not be relied upon.

The authorities and procedures that deal with change must therefore be arranged in such a way that it would be impossible for them to introduce elements detrimental to the coherence of the system as such. In order to achieve this they must be coherent in themselves and systematically connected with each other.

Thus we are led to a system of such authorities, as we were led to a system of codes before. And as an ultimate system of rules was necessary in the other case, an ultimate system of special provisions is needed where there are explicit and formalised ways of effecting change. *Such an ultimate system of authorities and their governing rules is the given community's legislative system.*

Not all communally significant rules, codes, etc. need to be subject to the legislative authority for there can exist independent rule bound structures, for example an actor's fan club, or the Greengrocers' Association, who might safely alter their structure in their own right. But in such cases (a) these are not an integral part of the communal structure, and (b) even then they are co-ordinated with the communal system in that the area of their independence is well defined. For instance, fan clubs, trade associations, etc. are not permitted to use jail sentences and death as penalties in their systems. This might not be a necessary restriction but obviously some such restrictions are essential to preserve the unity of the whole.

The unity and completeness of the legislative system can be ensured in one or another of two ways:

(i) *By having one ultimate authority.* (Hobbes thought this was the only way.)[4]

[4] Cf. T. Hobbes, *Leviathan* (1651). But he confused the legislative system with a system of government, of which we will speak later.

This consists in authorisation for all change coming from one source. In practice many forms are possible since authority can be exercised in diverse ways, for example: by approving or vetoing proposals; by reserving the right to countermand decisions; by announcing and supervising the execution of policies; etc.

It has to be noted that the existence of a central authority would not ensure the stability of the system unless whoever has the authority could be relied upon to try to keep the community stable. He or they could be formally charged with it by an appropriate policy maxim e.g. that communal stability is to be maintained and guarded.

In such a case there can be no authority to change this maxim. If there is no such rule, the assurance of stability and coherence in the system is no stronger than the belief in the good sense and reliability of those wielding the ultimate power, be they a man or a body of men. It might well be thought that such security is insufficient. This brings us to the second method.

(ii) *By having an ultimate system of regulations and maxims ensuring the desired stability.*

(a) By instituting a system of cross-checks between the separate legislative authorities in virtue of which a change proposed by one of them would have to be accepted by the others, or at least by those of the others whose areas of competence might be affected by the proposed alteration, that is, *rules of co-operation.*

(b) By promulgating general rules requiring the authorities to endeavour to keep the system coherent throughout the changes, that is, *rules of policy.*

(a) and (b) are of course independent, for it is possible to require co-operation without imposing a policy, and *vice versa.*

In the first case we still have to trust the good sense of those in authority, but we might well regard it as less likely that all of them should become irresponsible at the same time. Since the co-operation requirement would check the irresponsible tendencies of those who have them, these might never become dangerous.

The second case is more complex, for if the policy were to concern the coherence of the ultimate communal system, it is hard to see how the policy could be carried out without inter-authority co-operation, even if such co-operation is not required. The only exception being a system so simple that all coherence requirements are apparent to everybody. But then there would hardly be scope for the existence of different authorities.

As was argued before rules need not be enforced to be accepted – indeed, a direct acceptance of them is the foundation of any community.

Thus it could be argued that the different legislative authorities, and the people in authority could be expected to accept the necessary covenants "without sword". Consequently there might be no need for an ultimate authority. But there is a difficulty here. As long as standing arrangements are implicit and concern a large number of people of whom everyone accepts them independently, their own ponderousness gives them stability. If the rules are explicit, and concern a relatively small number of people, particularly those who have the authority to play with rules, the situation is changed. For it must be apparent to those subjected to the rules, that they need not be obeyed. Their good will is then the ultimate guarantee of the workability of the system, whereas in the other case the guarantee lay in the non-collusive acceptance of the rules by a number of different individuals.

Thus the more sophisticated the system, while more flexible and more satisfactory in many ways, the more it tends to bring its own perils with itself.

In fact various other arrangements to improve the situation can either grow with the system or be instituted.

(i) In a community there might grow a body of rules concerned with public-spiritedness; public, and public office, propriety; etc. A large number of things are simply not done, a number of attitudes are not displayed or even admitted by people who have, or would have, any standing in society. Those who contravene these rules are unlikely to go far or to be placed in positions of authority. For instance it simply does not cross the mind of the average Englishman that the public good could very well be a matter of complete indifference to his legislators, rulers and public servants, or that anyone with such an attitude could go far in a public career. In this way an implicit system of checks develops, which satisfyingly displays a ponderousness and stability of its own.

Such safeguards can work for it is hard to dodge an untidy mass of implicit reactions. But a skill can be developed in manipulating the conventional response, and explicit authority can be employed to achieve much in dealing with the recalcitrant residue. Foolproof assurance is more than can be hoped for, it is however desirable to have more than one insurance if none can be entirely reliable.

(ii) Let us illustrate another type of check by an example. It might be thought that the point made above, concerning the additional security derived from multiplicity of authorities, is of large significance. It is then possible to have division of power (authority) as a deliberate check, as an essential part of the system. The division can then be thought out and set up deliberately in order to enhance its check and security function. Thus we might have not merely different authorities, but authorities conceived in such a way that each exercises a salutary controlling influence on the others. Locke's division of power into legislative, judiciary and foreign affairs, and Montesquieu's into legislative, executive and judiciary, are best known examples of this method.[5]

One of the main functions of either of the systems lies in dividing the area of authoritative political decision in such a way that collaboration between independent authorities is necessary to bring about undesirable changes of such magnitude that disastrous consequences could follow. Legislation not supported by the executive and judiciary is useless – and exercise of executive power without the support of the judiciary and legislative basis is perilous and difficult. Legal action against laws and without executive or legislative support tends to be both futile and illegal.

Other and simpler security methods are often added to this. The mere selection of ultimate authorities is significant, thus democracies will not nominate the military as one of the ultimate powers, for reasons that are both compelling and obvious.

Still from our point of view the existence, the nature, and the advisability of such checks is of secondary importance. What is of prime interest is the possibility of the existence of, and the nature of, legislative authority and legislative systems, their basic function, specific character and their relation to other elements of communal structure. This we now have indicated.

It will be obvious that only minimal sophistication can be attained by a structure devoid of legislative arrangements, legislative authority procedures, and in fact a legislative system. It will be for instance clear that any body that deserves the name of state and any political community will be too complex to avoid this development. I cannot think of an obvious name to mark off the societies below and above this divide, and I do not think it is important to have one, though it might

[5] It has to be noted that these divisions embrace systems of government as well as legislative systems. Compare here: J. Locke, *On Civil Government* (1689) and Montesquieu, *The Spirit of the Laws*, (1748).

be convenient to call systems lacking legislative machinery *sub-political.* If this sounds artificial let us remark that natural names in this area are usually tied much more closely to practical matters and particular differences. Thus "dictatorship"; "constitutional government";"tribal structures"; etc. are typical appellations.

If we remember that legislative requirement can be very simply taken care of in simple dictatorship by vesting all power in the dictator or junta, we can see a reason for this terminological preference. Theoretically significant classifications can make remarkably little direct difference to practical style of life, which is the primary concern of the ordinary citizen.

Let us also remark that the existence of legislative arrangements is quite unlikely to be the only aspect of the difference between two different societies exemplifying the different levels of structural sophistication mentioned above. The next chapter deals with some of the other principal ones.

CHAPTER VIII

SOCIAL ENGINEERING: SYSTEMS OF GOVERNMENT

Legislative rules are concerned with methods and authorities empowered to deal with communal structure as such, and thus are *meta* or second order, their objects are the direct rules *viz.* the rules that control the business of living, living together, dealing with the contingencies and emergencies that arise, etc.[1]

In contradistinction the decisions taken by legislators i.e. the individuals or bodies empowered to introduce changes in the communal structure must needs both change and promulgate direct rules, whereby the actions of legislators can, and usually do have direct relevance to what is society's main and foremost concern. However, legislators *qua* legislators only make and promulgate rules and laws, they do not apply them in this capacity, though a single individual may of course have more than one official capacity.

There are rules that need not be explicitly applied, this happens if and when they, and a uniform interpretation of them, are internalised by all concerned e.g. the basic rules of a community. But this state of affairs is an exception rather than a rule where explicit and articulate arrangements are concerned, especially with respect to rules introduced by legislation. It is after all more than unlikely that a law and its interpretation should be internalised by all concerned due solely to the act of its promulgation. This then points to the need for an authority differing in character from the legislative.

Further, almost all the rules discussed above (with the exception of those discussed last) were directed towards dealing with the day to day needs of individual and communal life, but since the discussion was almost exclusively centred on standing arrangements, rules, etc.,

[1] Cf. here H. L. A. Hart, *The Concept of Law*, Ch. V, p. 78–9. Hart's distinction is different from the present one, but it is clear that it can be added with profit to it – for it will be obvious that social engineering is impossible without Hart's second type rules (conferring powers public or private) and society without his first type (imposing duties) even if these last are a bit narrowly concerned for the present purpose.

leaving aside changing and *ad hoc* contingencies, it was too narrow to be sufficient. Such arrangements can only establish what is, and what is not, expected etc. Thus they are limited to dealing with *recurring contingencies* as such and no other, and are not sufficient on their own deal with *ad hoc* contingencies, even where both the rule and its interpretation are internalised.

When immediate problems arise we can either deal with them unthinkingly or explicitly. That is, either we formulate the problem for ourselves and deal with it, or we merely react to it. Thus we could unthinkingly follow a set of rules,[2] or else we could act haphazardly. When people act haphazardly they are not organized, and there is no question of either co-operation or policy.

Clearly, given all the standing rules that might be necessary, immediate contingencies will arise that are not entirely covered. To start with some contingencies might be to all intents and purposes non-foreseeable and non-recurring. Further if e.g. a code of honour demands a duel in reply to an insult, many a time the question might be as to whether an insult in fact took place. Not all cases can be covered explicitly in any given code, and it is obvious that the problem of application of a rule to possible cases that might fall under it is in itself a recurring problem of a non-recurring nature: for the interpretation and the application-decision following on it are necessary precisely because the individuality of the particular case defies successful tabulation. *The case is always more particular than the rule allows for.* The point of general prescription lies in this that it does apply to a number of cases, otherwise it would establish no practice – it would be a *command* not a regulation. Often the decision is almost automatic and easy and obvious, sometimes it is extremely difficult, but it is always necessary.

Furthermore it is not desirable to have too many rules and regulations. If there are too many the system becomes quite rigid, and this is deplorable, if not downright dangerous. Excessive rigidity can more than counterbalance the benefits of communal co-operation. In fact some types of problems do, and *some do not lend themselves to handling in terms of standing arrangements and regulations.* Roughly a regulation can deal satisfactorily with the type of reaction required in the type of contingency, but not with a situation in which the reaction must be sensitively particular, rather than generalised. Courting techniques are

[2] I do not intend to imply that basic rules are a mere result of conditioning, much more they are a result of upbringing; they are not however articulated every time that they are followed.

never really satisfactory and almost always painfully obvious.

Such rules as: "Give assistance to people in danger"; "Always render medical help to those who need it"; etc. make sense. Such rules as: "Give artificial respiration to those who need medical help"; "In a case of a snake-bite, make an incision above the left elbow..."; or "When courting, say 'You are the most beautiful and witty person I have ever met'," are merely ridiculous.

There is a class of rules that seem to demand no interpretation at all, they are artificial in that they apply to contrived situations which because of their contrived nature can be uniform. An example is a rule such as: "Always stand to attention when a superior rank commands 'Attention'!" But even here exceptions are possible – e.g.: the private is under doctor's orders not to stand up; he is engaged in observing enemy movement and coming to attention would amount to a dereliction of this superior duty, etc. As these show, cases can arise where interpretation of even the most formalized rule becomes necessary.

The more general the directive the less chance there is that it might be inadequate for a possible case, but by the same token, it is less helpful and achieves less. Thus it is almost impossible to fault the directive to render medical help when needed, but it tells one nothing about what to do in any particular case – it merely bars indifference. In contradistinction, the rule :"If a man is bitten on the forearm, apply a tourniquet as near to the elbow as possible, then..." tells one a lot of what to do, but is applicable to only very few cases of snake bite, not to mention other medical contingencies.

A satisfactory set of rules must combine the achievement of maximum relevant direction with having relevance to the maximum number of possible cases.[3] Usually rules of different orders of generality operate together to achieve this elusive goal. Often too, rules are implemented by instructions, i.e. information and advice.

Lastly, it is impossible to foresee and to provide for all the possible contingencies, not only because some are unforeseeable but also because it is impossible to have rules to deal with every possible case in which a concerted communal action is desirable or, indeed, necessary.

Where reliance on rules is impractical it is possible to try to depend on the good sense of the individual members. If the Yeti were to attack a Himalayan community, some people would panic, but most might take

[3] This disregards the problem of those contingencies that are better left rule-free for one reason or another, for example a moral reason.

some *ad hoc* concerted action against them, and they might be successful in defending themselves if they do.

This has two drawbacks.

Firstly, the kind of action taken would be almost accidental. What was done would most probably be less adequate than it could be, people might do things in the wrong way, and there might not be enough of them. Very likely there might be a complete failure to co-operate effectively. Think here of a bush-fire – most communities faced with one will take some action, pour water, cut firebreaks, remove combustibles, etc., and this is better than doing nothing. But it might happen that not enough people concentrate on making a firebreak, rendering the other precautions futile. If the bush borders several communities, they might come into action when directly threatened by the fire, but it might be necessary for all to join at the first outbreak. How is that to be ensured?

Secondly, where a community is large and sophisticated, some contingencies might be too complex to lend themselves to any effective spontaneous actions. Those will be typically of communal concern and very often such that it would be either impracticable or impossible to have regulations to deal with them. How can these be dealt with?

The usual answer, and the correct one, is to *set up an authority*. There must be two aspects to such an authority:

(i) It has to be in a position to reach decisions and to direct others. An aspect of this will consist of the right to initiate action where rules in themselves do not prescribe any. Thus the Country Fire Authority can initiate burning off of grass; the cutting of firebreaks; alerts, etc.

(ii) It is usually charged with a responsibility whose scope is understood. One aspect of this will consist of it having a certain sovereignty in the matter of some type of contingency and certain areas of communal co-operation. Thus the Country Fire Authority can not only initiate action regarding fires, but it has the last say on what should and what should not be done regarding them. Another aspect will usually involve a policy imposed on the authority. Thus the Country Fire Authority is expected in the first place to do everything possible to prevent fires, and if they cannot be prevented, to fight them as effectively as possible.

Unless there is only one authority complexities are likely to arise, e.g.:

several authorities might be involved in the same type of contingency. Thus since water is used to fight fires, if there is a separate Water Board, it will be *nolens volens* involved in fire fighting. There could be sectional authorities of the same kind. Their responsibilities and competence could cross. If unified and efficient action is to be ensured, a system of authorities will have to arise, in terms of which mutual relations of the different bodies and men (in authority) are set out and determined.

This point was discussed in the last Chapter with respect to the legislative system, which is but a system of authorities-cum-rules, whose responsibility it is to adapt the explicit communal structure to the changing demands put on it. So here too a hierarchy of authorities and rules determining their mutual relations will find their place. And here too it will usually be the combination of both that will determine the ultimate nature of the system of authorities.

The policy aspect too can be quite complex, different aspects of the policy might be the responsibility of separate bodies within the system of authority. Furthermore, policies as well as rules need both interpretation and adaptation, and on their own will not determine actions with any precision. Often an action in terms of a policy might change or determine the policy, not merely apply it, thus quite possibly bringing administration in conflict with legislation. This is illustrated very clearly by court practice. Lawyers habitually refer to cases and decisions as often as to codes, for in terms of the same code, different decisions might mean entirely different policies.[4] Sometimes legislative action is taken to implement or reverse court practice.

But often it is advisable to leave more of policy-making responsibility explicitly in the hands of a responsible authority, this being for various reasons. Let us only mention the fact that a body whose business it is to control health and hygiene, will soon acquire a body of knowledge and practical skill in the area. They will come to know what is most dangerous, what steps are most effective, what dangers are most prevalent, etc. Obviously they are in a much better position to formulate a policy to be followed in the area than others. It might well be best left to them to determine it. This has to be understood to be a presumption, not a law of nature; instances to the contrary unhappily

[4] This is well illustrated by constitutional law cases for constitutions are notoriously difficult to alter and legal interpretation fills the gap thus created. *Vide* e.g.: The Australian so-called Engineers Case – Amalgamated Society of Engineers *v.* Adelaide Steamship Co. Ltd. (1920) 28 C.L.R. 129.

abound, but let us not confuse uses and abuses of things. *We can* limit ourselves mainly to the first. Such are the splendours of an investigation in principle.

The danger here lies in the natural tendency of such a body towards high-handedness. They might not know where the shoe pinches and they might care even less. It is particularly the case that marginal benefits and inconveniences are often treated with scant respect and the satisfactoriness of the system suffers. Yet such an attitude is no more than the natural consequence of being in authority.

Separate authorities or systems of authorities could thus exist for the purpose of dealing with practical problems arising in separate areas, or with respect to different classes of contingency. But what held of rules, and of legislative rules and authorities, holds also for practical authorities. Thus actions of one can and often will support, nullify or limit the actions of another. For instance, the Water Board could reduce the water-pressure and nullify the Fire Brigade's effort in fighting a bushfire.

When the situation is very simple, and the practical actions in the community are generally determined by common sense, it is possible to envisage a few separate authorities with fairly separate functions.[5] When, however, the situation is complex, authorities can hardly be unencumbered by others in the exercise of their functions.

In such a situation there is an obvious need for an ultimate system of administrative systems. Such an ultimate system is the community's system of government.

This use of "government" is slightly wider than the ordinary use because it does not require that a system of government should feature a central co-ordinating agency or a central authority, *viz.* the government.

Once administrative authorities exist, the rules can not only prescribe what should be done and establish rights, duties, liberties and privileges, but also *permit or require that certain matters should be referred to certain authorities.* Thus disputes can be settled out of court, but might be taken to court. Matters of criminal nature have to be taken to court, and happily this cannot be done with ordinary family quarrels. Authorities and institutions can have different status. A court of petty sessions can deal with petty matters only, and can be over-

[5] In some cases the areas of authority could be in fact completely separate. Thus for instance actions of a snow-clearing authority can hardly come in contact with the activities of the mid-summer festival authority.

ridden by a higher court, but not *vice versa*. Many similar examples can be given without difficulty.

Taken simple-mindedly, the above account could be misleading, for it draws distinctions between: status positions; rules; codes; systems of rules; of legislative authority; of government and administration; authority and governing rules; policy-making and policy implementation; areas of responsibility, etc. These distinctions are valid and one hopes illuminating, but they could be taken as indicating that all phenomena of communal and social intercourse are tightly compartmentalised. They are not. The various problems shade into each other and the same is true about the various methods employed to deal with them – still the main differing features are clearly distinguishable. For instance, the system of government is different in character from the legislative system. The second must be comprehensive – all changes in the social system that can be made explicitly must be provided for in the system,[6] for all explicit communal rules must be a part of the ultimate coherent system on the pain of creation of anarchy.

The only case in which anarchy need not arise from absence of the overall system is one where the separate and not dovetailed authorities *fail to be significantly related*. Thus there could exist an after-life directorate dealing with funeral rites; and ordinary directorate dealing with food, defence, etc. and a sickness and weakness directorate dealing with those unfit for ordinary life and as yet not dead – independent to all intents and purposes, and sovereign in their spheres. The respective legislation could be separate as well for the contingencies they deal with obviously differ in kind. Yet even in this case, as soon as an attempt by one of the authorities to claim competence in another area is seriously made, a system becomes urgently necessary. Furthermore the example is highly artificial and the artificiality appears inescapable for in all normal cases arrangements are connected. Given this the business of legislative authorities is naturally also interconnected and must form a system that could be untidy in a marginal way only, otherwise many decisions or implications of decisions would come to contradict each other, and the communal structure would be subjected to an intolerable strain.

The account is different with practical matters that arise whether or not they are subject to arrangements. Provided only that the rules in the group are comprehensive enough to make the group into a community, there could be a large number of areas of possible inter-indivi-

[6] Only very small contraventions of this principle can be absorbed by a communal system.

dual action that might not be regarded as of communal concern and consequently might fail to be provided for in standing communal rules. Thus the system of administration need not be comprehensive, for matters that might very well be a subject of social administration might be left unattended to. For instance, matters administered by the state in a socialist system are left open in a *laissez faire* society. As a community grows bigger and its structure becomes more complex, it naturally grows more comprehensive, but there are those who resist the change, for example, in the name of free enterprise. Despite their opposition the process is to some extent inevitable – in our society private roads, water supply, mints, etc. are not possible – a point noted by K. Galbraith.[7] Sometimes communal control goes further than sheer necessity dictates. It is a matter of much heated controversy whether this is a good thing – it seems reasonable to assume that in some cases it is, and in others it is not. At any rate even the free actions of individuals must be subject to certain limits imposed where they come into contact with controlled areas; obviously in a more sophisticated set-up there are more controls and fewer areas of wide freedom can remain. Our solace lies in the fact that the area of possible human actions is indefinitely large.

It might appear that both administrative and legislative possibilities are fully circumscribed. This because all administrative arrangements must have their legislative backing if the situation is sophisticated enough. However there exist possible governmental problems that are not seen as such simply because the administrative system does not deal with them. Thus in Tudor England the government did not deal with: public transport, postal services, health, old age and sickness provisions, customs, passports and entry permits, etc., yet these were possible areas of civil administration, and are now actually the province of government. Nowadays the legislative system has to back up these arrangements and authorities *because they exist* and have ramifications that are significant in terms of other elements of control. It could be claimed with plausibility that an indefinitely large number of areas of governmental control can be thought up even if all of them could not co-exist in the one community. A problem is created thereby for the legislative system, for a novel and unusual set-up could be proposed at any moment, and it might escape not only any existing legal provision but also the control of any known legislative authority as defined.

Such crises have been known to arise and create problems; these are

[7] Cf. K. Galbraith, *The Affluent Society*, Hamish Hamilton, 1958.

akin to competence disputes between British Unions that unhappily are wont to arise whenever a new type of job comes into existence. On a more sophisticated level we usually find an authority empowered to deal with such cases – that is, having the power to legislate for all, so to say, unclassified contingencies that demand this kind of action. It could be a separate authority or it could be vested in another one as an addition to its other competence. It could even have a form of a system where possibilities are divided according to their kind – but then competence disputes are likely to arise and have to be solved.

The existence of such a novelties-authority will contribute towards the stability of the legislative system. The system of government does not need one.[8] For here even if the new areas can be very different and novel, where they clearly infringe on an existing structure they can be incorporated in it, *viz.* uranium prospecting with other traditional mining, or mining on the moon with space administration; where they do not they need not be administered, and even if they are, they might stay separate like air and road traffic controls. The significant connections being pragmatic not conceptual. At any rate the unity of the legislative system is sufficient to ensure that new ventures will fit, for when the need for control arises or changes, as when the motor car or aeroplane become more than promising toys, legislation will provide for the existence of the necessary administrative authority and will harmonise it with the rest of the system – more cannot be required in advance of any development.

The system of government as such consists in appropriate authorities and their governing rules, much as does the system of legislation.

The governing rules determine the relations between, and the competence of, the responsibility,[9] the power, etc., of the various authorities. They can be used in both cases[10] to ensure smooth and satisfactory working of the system and its elements. In the case of the administrative system however, less emphasis is placed on the coherence of the decisions, and more on their direct satisfactoriness. In both cases coherence and co-operation can be ensured by a hierarchic system of authority, thus an ultimate authority might have the power to direct all others, countermand their decisions, etc.

As always it is of interest to the community that the system should

[8] It should be remembered that in practice governing bodies will often carry their own legislative machinery, in many cases a welcomed sophistication. A mixed or a partially mixed system ensues.

[9] *Viz.*, duties, policies to implement, etc.

[10] I.e. Legislative and Administrative.

be not only workable, but also satisfactory,[11] and analogous problems of ensuring the best possible state of affairs will arise with respect to both systems. Lastly, the systems are not independent of each other since the nature of the administrative one is determined by the actions of the legislative one, legislative problems can be created by administrative practices, and quite obviously the authorities can be combined.

A system of government can be entirely authority directed. In such a case all the controls are in terms of the ultimate authority, that usually works through a hierarchy of lesser authorities. It could be understood that the ultimate power can, even if it need not, interfere on any level and countermand or refuse to ratify any decision; any lesser authority could be taken to proceed from the ultimate source and to continue at its pleasure. Furthermore, in a pure case the authority could be absolute also in the sense that no rules were regarded as limiting it, imposing a policy on it, specifying its duties, etc. Thus theoretically there could be no limits to its power. To make the case complete the authority could be absolute both in the administrative and in the legislative spheres.

The above is *a logically pure case of totalitarianism.* It is impossible for such an arrangement to exist in practice in any sophisticated community. For where we have a *complex rule structure* we must have a *system of operating it,* and *that must exclude capriciousness* as a principle.

Thus a system is not viable when the whim of any man or body of men is the only determining factor. This is so, for unless ways and means of achieving results and of implementing decisions are standardised and therefore prescribed, the system is not workable. I am not, by the way, maintaining that it is impossible for a tyrant to make private policy decisions and to, say, decide privately that the law has been changed. This he could do – what is more, he could impose his will in that he might require the courts to decide in accordance with what was in his mind even though it was not known to anybody else at the time.[12] What I am maintaining is that if a tyrant were to act in such a way on a great many occasions he might, if he is lucky and skilful, continue to have hegemony over the community, but to a large extent *he would have ceased to use its legal* system – its complete abuse puts it in abeyance and makes it unworkable if it is known that such abuse shall continue.

[11] I take "satisfactory" to mean something like satisfactory to a majority in most ways. If it is satisfactory to the ruling clique at the cost of others, I would not call it communally satisfactory, but would rather say that the community is used by another group or a sub-group.

[12] He could announce what it was at the trial. Thus a certain proportion of capriciousness could be tolerated by the system.

But the Courts could still be used, albeit as agencies: dispensing the will of the tyrant; satisfying his love of pomp and formality; bamboozling the simple-minded or the outside-form worshippers, etc.

But even in a most severe case, there is a limit to the capriciousness that a tyrant can display, for it is impossible in a community of any size to have no system of control at all. Should all the decisions be completely capricious, there would be no standing expectations left. If there are no standing expectations, there can be no standing arrangements. If there are no standing arrangements there are no rules. In such circumstances if anyone wishes to exert any control he must do it *ad hoc* and by direct force – and this method has severe limitations well presented in Hobbes' "State of Warre."[13] To put it in a nutshell, to control a community one has to have a community but there can be none in the absence of standing expectations.

This can be concealed by the fact that we generally think of governmental and/or tyrannical control as control in terms of the superstructure and its explicit rules, and take it for granted that the basic rules of the sub-structure suffice to form the community in question. In a sophisticated set-up this may be insufficient, in any case – if all decisions in the sphere of the superstructure are capricious – there is no superstructure and no control on this level. Since this is the only control a tyrant can have, he has no control. Even a tyrant has to operate a system of communal control and this requires predictability.

To operate a system one has to work largely within it, hence those who wish to use it must accept it and then they become bound by it in a formal but significant way. The thing that they can manipulate most easily is the policy implemented by the system, although there are very real limits even to this.[14] An exception to this might be found in a very small and simple community. There the tyrant and the will of the tyrant might be easily known to all and thus be directly operative, but even a sophisticated community can become very authoritarian within practical limits imposed by the formal structure of the communal system.

From this "summit" communal systems can be ranged progressively towards less totalitarian authority and more communal safeguard. The ultimate case would consist in maximum reliance on governing rules and minimum employment of authority. In such a case the governing rules would narrowly prescribe: what policies are to be followed; what aims are to be selected; what adjustments are to be made for what purpose,

[13] T. Hobbes, *Leviathan*.

[14] As Marx has clearly seen. Cf. *The Eighteenth Brumaire of Louis Bonaparte*.

etc. A pure system of this kind, where the character of the community is absolutely prescribed by governing rules would be *the ultimate in constitutionalism.*

In its very nature constitutionalism cannot be logically pure, for to become so it would have to bar any free decision by any authority whatever, thus making authority a mere agency. However, as we argued above, this is quite impossible, for it is impossible to foresee all future contingencies, thus every explicit system of administration and legislation must make use of some authority or authorities that can deal with the unforeseen. We could try to find an example where in such cases the community relies on the commonsensical reaction of its members. But then the unguided commonsense of the majority (or its chance reaction) assume the mantle of the ultimate political authority. The less that is left to an authority or authorities, and the lesser the level of possible authoritative decision, the closer the system will approximate to ultimate constitutionalism.

There are many ways of approaching the constitutionalist ideal. Authorities could be compartmentalised and the common effect of their decisions determined by application of governing rules. Authoritative decisions might be limited to lower levels and their effect on higher level rules might be determined by application of special rules. Authorities could be prevented from making decisions whenever possible, instead they could be given the power to suggest courses of action, the decisions to be determined by application of appropriate rules designed to decide between different suggestions and suggestions of different authorities. Electronic computers offer many fancy possibilities in this field.

The obvious and insurmountable problem lies in that, in this system, if pure, there is no way in which something completely unforeseen can be dealt with for no one has the right to take a free decision on behalf of the community. As a reply it could be maintained either: (a) that where the constitution is silent, we have a liberty (*viz.* a right to free action); or (b) that all contingencies are in fact allowed for in the constitution, and all that remains to be done is to subsume them correctly under the relevant rule i.e. to put it in a legal form. It must be a matter of principle that every possible case is capable of such interpretation. This supreme legal fiction could be regarded as sacrosanct.

There are problems with both the suggestions. *Ad* (a): With the passage of time as conditions change more and more of people's activity will be in the liberty area – these actions would have ramifications with respect to many forms of communal life – it is doubtful whether a large area of anarchy would combine well with organised communal life. *Ad* (b): If an issue has repercussions in communal life (and everything is likely to have), it comes under the constitution. But this relevance cannot guarantee that an obviously relevant regulation exists. These must be provided, and since the task would be endless the problem is either not solved or its weight shifts to interpretation of the existing rules. But given the problems outlined above those who have the right of interpretation will *in fact* assume both the administrative and the legislative power, as often happens for this very reason with guardians of Holy Scriptures.

The usual answer to this type of difficulty is to have a general rule, or rules, and an interpretative authority – a court, a referendum, a parliamentary Royal Commission, etc. But then how is the giving of such an interpretation different from reaching an administrative or legislative decision as the case may be? If a rule is really general more than one interpretation will be equally defensible on formal grounds – the court *decides* the right one, it *does not find it,* at best it decides between those that it finds correct. A disguised decision making is nonetheless decision making, and it might be cumbersome because it is disguised.[15]

In practice of course, we seldom if ever strive towards complete constitutionalism. It is hardly likely to be satisfactory. No more satisfactory in fact than a completely totalitarian system would be. In the latter case however, those in authority barrack for it and often find it attractive. So it has some defenders, but in fact we always find a combination of the two systems. This mixture will tend one way or the other and bear different names.

In those terms many different systems could exist. To discern, name and describe them is not however the job of a philosopher, it is the province of political science, political theory and/or sociology.

I have sought to distinguish a legislative system and a system of government, one was designed to deal with the very structure of the community where this structure was explicit, the other was administrative in that it was designed to deal with all other contingencies that could face the group.

A combination of the two systems I will call the political system of the community. This will of course comprise, as it must, all administrative

[15] The history of legal interpretations of the U.S. Constitution provides a useful illustration here.

and legislative machinery, *viz.* governing rules and authorities capable of dealing, and/or necessary to deal, with any problem, any contingency and any need of the community, seen as such.[16]

The two systems need not be separate, for one system might be capable of dealing with both administrative and legislative problems. Here they were considered as distinct because this separates the structural and organisational elements thus enhancing clarity of exposition. There is also another reason for it. The system of administration is different from problems of administration. Clearly the system itself will create problems, but these are essentially of indirect import, that is, they concern ways in which we might deal with other problems. It is advisable then in practice to think of them as a special class since they might, and usually will, require different types of handling and different types of consideration might be significant in thinking about them.[17]

If we wish we can divide the area of political administration quite differently. A number of considerations might lead us to adopt this, that or another division. Often they will be practical. Take as an example Montesquieu's[18] division of powers into Legislative, Executive and Judiciary. Judiciary is the other power. It is essentially an authority by reference to which we obtain independent interpretations of the law and decisions as to what is the import of this or that type of rule in cases where an explicit decision is either formally or practically necessary. In our terminology it is then an element of the system of government, albeit clearly distinguished from all others and enjoying autonomy on a par with the legislative and executive (*viz.* the residue of governmental) powers. Also it can assume virtual legislative powers in the circumstances mentioned above.

The distinction is clearly intelligible, but so would others be; consider here for example, Locke's power of external affairs,[19] and powers to deal with such things as: education; religious beliefs; transport; defence; to name only a few.

The point of Montesquieu's distinction lies in providing a check against authoritarian and high-handed governmental attitudes. Its effectiveness lies in driving a wedge between legislation and administration and in removing to a large extent the possibility of the executive assuming

[16] This qualification allows for lack of administrative, etc. control of an enterprise or an action or a contingency that yet could be of real communal importance, such as, for example, the carrying of firearms, provided only that it is thought of as a private matter.

[17] Cf. here H. L. A. Hart, "Primary and Secondary Rules," Ch. V, *The Concept of Law.* The point raised by Hart is somewhat similar.

[18] *The Spirit of the Laws.*

[19] *On Civil Government.*

legislative powers by means of interpretation. This is a great danger as is evidenced time and again in political history. Hence the system enjoys deservedly a widespread recognition.

Having noted these possibilities we shall move on because they are really out of place in prolegomena such as these, for they are theoretical in argument but closely practical in their import and intention.

A political system exists if, and only if, all the "independent" constituent systems, if any, form one ultimate structure.

This is achieved automatically where there is only one total system. Where there are several, they must be joined. At the very least the mutual relations, relative competence, etc., of the various systems must be formally determined, either in terms of governing rules, or through an arbitrating authority, or both. This can be quite complex for if, e.g. there are the L-system and the G-system, the rules could specify for example, that in cases of α, β, γ, Δ etc., the L-system is the interpretative and final authority, and in cases a, b, c, d, etc. it is the G-system. It could add that cases x, y, z, etc. are to be decided and/or allocated by a special body S (the Supreme Court, the government, etc.) and so on.

The main point is that there must be a definitive and final way of deciding any problem that might concern both authorities, any dispute that can arise between them, and so on.[20] This is the same type of requirement that pointed to the necessity of codes, not merely rules; systems, not merely codes; and an ultimate system given any community, not merely a number of separate systems. Unless there is a unified system of rule and authority, there cannot exist an ultimate system, and the community cannot have a unified group structure.

This then completes the sketch of communal structure attempted in this book, it is of course far from complete, but enough was said to give an indication of the method advocated, and of the nature of the problems, if it leads to further discussion the work would have fulfilled its purpose.

[20] This point was large in the mind of Hobbes. Compare here also Chapter VII.

APPENDIX

SOME GENERAL REMARKS ON PLURALISM AND THE RELATIVE SATISFACTORINESS OF SYSTEMS OF POLITICAL CONTROL[1]

A system of political control is satisfactory if an ultimate community organized according to the system is safe, i.e. has sufficient stability, and if in addition to this it provides for the satisfaction of all essential needs in the community, and pays further special attention to basic needs. It is a good system if it also confers benefits with respect to as many of the other needs and desires as possible, possibly in the order of their respective merit.[2]

It is our present task to offer a short preliminary analysis of this problem. The remarks that follow are made without prejudice to the hitherto expounded theory, which is independent of them, and of course powerless to challenge the results of any proper empirical inquiry in these matters. It is hoped that this attempt might *inter alia* illustrate how the above theoretical considerations *could turn out* when applied to actual situations, conditions and people. It will be assumed that people are motivated by the broad well-known and prevalent considerations. These will be regarded as influencing their attitudes to the communities in which they live and systems of political control will be assessed by reference to these attitudes.

We can plausibly say that a good system must be at least satisfactory, but even this modest dictum can be challenged.[3] Hitler, for instance, would sacrifice satisfactoriness at least with respect to some citizens for the glory of the German millennium, he regarded the Nazi system as good for in his opinion it led to such a millennium. From time to time others make similar claims. To apply to such a system organized to meet this type of aim the word "good" is strictly speaking incorrect, and

[1] I mean a method of organizing a political system, or a political community, not the political system itself as defined in Chapter VIII above.

[2] Cf. here p. 136 above, Chapter VI.

[3] From now on I shall not indicate pedantically when I speak of a system of political control, when speaking of a political system organized according to it; the context should make the meaning clear. I shall generally use "political system" in most cases.

the point should be rather put by claiming that having an unsatisfactory system in the present time is justified in terms of future achievement, or even necessitated by it. To dispute or defend this point of view is not the purpose of this discussion, for it is concerned with what a good system is. However it should be noted that such a claim is not necessarily false, even if it tends to be implausible.

We could claim plausibly:

Firstly, that if one system leaves fewer basic, though non-essential needs unsatisfied than another, it will be to that extent more satisfactory, i.e. better.

COROLLARY: It seems permissible to omit here the essential needs, since their satisfaction is the condition of survival and perforce they must be satisfied with respect to the vast majority of the citizens. It could be argued that a system might permit a proportion of its subjects to perish – and survive itself – the galleys are witness to the fact that this is possible. It would appear unnecessary to claim nowadays that this is insufficient. It is at any rate permissible to assume that any satisfactory system must try to cater at the very least for the survival of all members of the community in question.

Secondly, that one system is more satisfactory than another if it provides for the satisfaction of more non-basic and non-essential needs than the other, i.e. if it confers more benefits than the other.

Here it should be noted that besides objective needs people tend to have: convictions; some conception of what their needs are; and some views concerning the relative importance of what they conceive of as their needs. These need not be, and in fact are not, the same for all people. Given the further fact that people's convictions lead them to adopt different goals not necessarily or directly related to their real needs, and indeed sometimes opposed to them, it becomes obvious that a simple assessment is unlikely to meet the case. This can be illustrated by citing a materialistic businessman, a Catholic missionary, and a Moslem evangelist. Their convictions differ – the businessman puts gain at the top of the importance scale, the other two subjugate it to what they call spiritual values, for example, the winning of converts – but their goals again differ, each tries to convert to a different religion. Further, one might accept brain-washing as an acceptable method, the other might not; one might place value on uniformity, another on sincerity, etc. To make the matter more complex some "values" become values if and when people regard them as such. How then is one to obtain a scale of needs and their importance against which to check the satisfactoriness of a political system?

Usually when a man says that a political system is good, he means to indicate that it accords with *his* values, ideals, goals, and *his* idea of the proper fulfilment of people's need-satisfaction, but this cannot pretend to objectivity.

An ideal society could be required to satisfy all real and felt "need requirements" of all its citizens. Since these can contradict each other this is utopian. They contradict each other often enough simply because people have uniformity as their goal. A religious person might wish for exclusively Christian, exclusively Buddhist or exclusively Catholic marriage law, an atheist might opt for registry marriage only, a pluralist might advocate a choice for everybody. These cannot be satisfied together in the one community, thus insistence on uniformity makes it impossible to have felt satisfactoriness for all citizens in cases where there are differences between them. As a remedy uniformity in all matters from all citizens could be required as the condition of their acceptance as citizens. This requirement does not appear reasonable where a community is concerned, for we are concerned with a group the membership of which is not voluntary but in practice obligatory for most individuals concerned; what is more it is likely to affect a great many of their actions and the majority of their relations with others. The problem of acceptance of prospective citizens on the basis of complete conformity becomes obvious when the fate of those who naturally differ in outlook is considered. If they cannot be changed, should they be imprisoned, banished or what?

It is of course possible to imprison, banish or execute people, the question is when it is justifiable and when not. Someone who is a danger to others must be restrained for obvious reasons but should we restrain a man who does not accept our view with respect to the relative importance of personal and common goals and aims particularly when our choice is subject to dispute, and where both aims can be pursued alongside each other?

For our purpose the main question is what is the basic aim of communal life? It is of course possible to band together in order to pursue a specific goal – such are: the potholers' club; the Methodist Church; the philatelic union; etc. For these groups it is quite proper to make the pursuance of the respective goals (or main goals) the *conditio sine qua non* of membership. But it will be clear that no such single goal is a *ratio existendi* of a community – not all communities have the same aims – but all philatelic societies collect stamps. All communities however provide a *modus vivendi* whereby all their citizens can live peacefully together, this is their primary function.[4] Further, if we disregard uniformity desires, it is in fact possible to achieve such a *modus vivendi* while allowing for divergence of goals, aims and convictions. Consequently to insist on uniformity amounts to the refusal to satisfy or to permit the seeking of the satisfaction of at least some needs of some of the citizens where there is no real necessity to do so in so far as community *qua* community is concerned and where such needs are in fact satisfiable. If this is to be justified reasons must be given. It is clear that the envisaged system would permit an extra satisfaction to some at the expense of lack of satisfaction by others. This has two practical drawbacks:

(a) it creates inter-citizen tension reflecting on the standard of internalisation of communal arrangements, and
(b) leaves some individuals needlessly dissatisfied in depth – for it is worse to be prohibited from e.g. following one's religion, than to be merely forced to accept the fact that some people follow something else.

Ad (a): The inter-individual tension created by a desire, or even more by a directive requiring uniformity is *in principle unresolvable* – the point of view of the uniformity representative cannot be accommodated with any view that differs fom his line, not only with the views of other uniformists. From the communal point of view this is a serious matter – here is a wish that cannot be adopted by a section of the participants. Yet as has been shown above community ultimately rests on internalised arrangements, thus a system that leads to unavoidable alienation of some individuals is for that reason weaker. If it be claimed that thwarting of uniformity desire can lead to such an alienation too the reply is that this is the lesser evil, and that at any rate it is only this one desire that will be thwarted, whereas in a uniformist society a whole spectrum of aims and desires would suffer. It is also the case that in the first instance only those who desire uniformity will be thwarted, and that to some extent for they can still follow their desire themselves. In practice of course uniformist arrangements though secondary *vis-à-vis* internalised ones are workable, but tend to weaken the communal fabric. Again in practice a community can absorb such tensions to a large degree. But the fact remains that even in practice such expectations and arrangements are alien to the com-

[4] This will be also seen from the account of community given in Chapter I.

munal enterprise for cooperation is both the point and the basis of it. Communal structure has to carry an uniformity directive as a burden, and if the number of the dissidents is large and their views strong the burden can be considerable. The point I wish to stress here is that a wish for uniformity of goals and aims – i.e. for what might be called ideological uniformity, tends in principle to be anti-social, for it is in principle difficult to reconcile it with communal aims and fabric *par excellence,* and an arrangement requiring uniformity of aim is always parasitic on communal cohesion achieved by other means. Other wishes are of course also capable of generating interpersonal tensions, but if uniformity is not aimed at, these differences can be, at least in principle, accommodated.[5]

Ad (b): The second point is also important, but it might be controversial in that people may try to justify the price of uniformity by reference to *higher* goods. Since there is obviously no agreement on this, the imposition of uniformity in the name of such a putative higher principle, amounts to the assumption of near infallibility on the part of the enforcer – hardly a reasonable stand.

Thus we come to a view that it is not desirable and it is socially disruptive to try to implement a wish for ideological uniformity. On the other hand it has to be admitted that any arrangements designed to accommodate differences in aims, preference, goals, etc. within one community must lead to complexities and some strain between those with different aims vying for the same resources.

Those who see the solution in uniformity can attempt to avoid this whole issue by recommending that laws should be enacted and/or regarded as valid *only where all citizens in fact accord.* This was the idea behind Rousseau's general will.[6] In such a case there is no guarantee that the uniform accord will concern matters and areas sufficient to make a community possible. Furthermore dissenters can arise where previously there were none. This would render laws void, since as soon as someone had a real wish to break them they would cease to exist for that reason alone. Even if it was demanded that the opposition to an arrangement should be opposition in principle before it renders it defunct, the laws could not retain sufficient stability, for conscientious objectors would not only be immune to them, but would render them inoperative for all others as well.

[5] It will be clear that I am here in complete disagreement with Devlin, *The Enforcement of Morals.* In fact the present argument tends to show that this position is fundamentally mistaken.

[6] J. J. Rousseau, *The Social Contract.*

Another possible palliative consists in tying uniform action to the wishes of the majority. In defence of this we can claim that at least the majority will always be satisfied. The composition of the majority on different issues is likely to be different, so anyone can expect to be dissatisfied some of the time, but he can also expect to be satisfied at least sometimes, and perhaps this is as good as we can expect.[7] But how is the wish of the majority to be determined in a complex society? It is impossible to take a vote on each and every issue, and once decision-making is either delegated to authorities or entrusted to faithful application of rules, difficulties arise. For instance the opportunity for full consideration on every issue cannot be given to all for obvious reasons. It would not be fair to hold people to their ill-considered marginal opinions formed on accidentally picked up scraps of information, yet a large proportion of actual views on almost any issue merits this description. The mere intention to accept the view of the majority is not enough, but a sufficient knowledge and even the existence of reliable majority opinion can be extremely dubious, and even where such opinions exist and are known they might bear insufficient relation to reality. It should be noted that these problems are most acute with respect to possible uniform opinions.

Further difficulties for the majority idea arise out of minority needs, wishes and convictions.[8] The somewhat Utopian democratic ideal is to have all satisfied all the time. The worst crime against it is to prevent completely and in principle the satisfaction of any need. Needs that can be satisfied in appropriate circumstances but happen to be thwarted on this or that occasion are a blemish, but those that are forever relegated to remain unfulfilled are a permanent liability of the system. Yet if all decisions are majority-bound, a number of possible needs and notably the needs of deviant people are likely to be relegated to this category. Well-known cases are those of the homosexuals and polygamists; but not so long ago left-handed people were also discriminated against.

Constitutionalism, a system where the stress is on rules and agreements is chiefly concerned with proper and communally agreed ways and means of putting ideas into practice.[9] By providing a fair machinery

[7] When the majority becomes a political party it becomes a body whose members are likely to display uniformity on most issues; here I talk of deciding issues on a separate majority count *vis-à-vis* every separate decision, i.e. an *ad hoc* majority.

[8] I am deliberately refraining from regarding them as rights.

[9] For a constitutionalist approach in traditional form see A. D. Lindsay, *The Modern Democratic State*, Oxford, 1943, and A. B. Gibson, "Nature and Convention in a Democratic State," *Australasian Journal of Philosophy*, 1951.

whereby people can have their ideas accepted it is hoped that interested and well-informed people can have relatively more influence for, where appropriate to the type of case, lobbying, forming of associations, putting up of proposals and cases in many different ways can be allowed for. These might succeed even if proposed by and representing a minority if they gain the proper acceptance. For example, if there is no protest from the majority; or if a special need or competence is suitably demonstrated; or on the strength of their argument; or on compassionate grounds, etc. Thus, given suitable circumstances, any wish has in principle a chance to be satisfied, even if some are less likely than others to be satisfied in fact.

This is attractive but not ideal, for it is easy to conceive of a constitutionalist system that will work smoothly and produce unsatisfactory results. In a community of any size and sophistication it is not an easy matter to find the right law to frame, the correct policy to adopt, etc. It is also the case that complex arrangements are more easily abused than simple ones e.g. the simple majority rule. It is clear that for instance lobbying and forming of associations can be used against the legitimate aspirations of others. Hitler's rise to power provides an ample illustration of this fact, so this is not a foolproof method of remedying the ills of the situation.

These points are often regarded as a sufficient argument against democracy and are in fact an argument that shows its weakness. However, disregarding the wishes of the people does not offer any obvious solution to the problem at hand while creating difficulties of its own. Clearly to disregard people's wishes is not the same as having their needs more effectively satisfied. What is more, and significant, people will not regard themselves as well served unless laws and arrangements are directed towards the satisfaction not only of their needs but also of their aspirations and wants.

It will be easily agreed that *needless* interference with the wants and wishes of others is not desirable and this can provide guidelines regarding permissible limits of law enactment. But the question what interference is legitimate is not easily settled. In a pure Millean case *the protection of others is the sole legitimate cause of coercion and limitation of people's freedom. Prima facie* this seems a reasonable ideal, yet not all accept it. Among others H.J. McCloskey[10] criticises this approach, e.g. on the point of feasibility. This is a legitimate worry, yet a Mill-

10 "The Problem of Liberalism," *The Review of Metaphysics*, 1965, and "Mill's Liberalism," *Philosophical Quarterly*, 1963.

type view need not be devastated by it. The essay *On Liberty* can be seen as contracting to three points; (*a*) that no one thinks of the loss of freedom as a good, though some think of it as a dispensable good; (*b*) that therefore a good reason is needed for any restriction of liberty; and (*c*) that the only good ground for such a restriction is to make the restricted person livable with.

There are problems even with this, provided for instance by drug-taking, where people's freedom is likely to result in grave physical damage to themselves, and there is little doubt about it. In view of such cases it might be necessary to amend clause (*c*) of the above dictum, but even so the position seems to contain an important truth. In any case it seems clearly permissible to accept it as the basis of discussion; the denial of satisfaction where satisfaction is possible always needs good reasons, since the whole purpose of communal association is the satisfaction of needs.[11] To qualify this it must be observed that some demands and/or needs can fail to have any standing. For instance if the satisfaction of someone's desire to be an important military figure would need a war, the ambition would be illegitimate even if it could be demonstrated that its satisfaction is personally essential to the man. Furthermore contradictory needs cannot be provided for together. As a rule of thumb principle it can be said that: ordinary, everyday and basic needs should take precedence over extraordinary, special, non-essential *viz.* dispensable ones. It is also clear that actual present satisfaction of present needs should be accorded more respect than the hypothetical future satisfaction of envisaged needs, and that for obvious reasons.

The main difficulty comes with the interpretation of legitimate cause to interfere or deny. Various claims are made on moral, religious, cultural, radical, national and idealistic grounds. Thus it could be and in fact was claimed that for example, divorce and homosexuality are morally wrong and should be repressed for that reason, similarly with atheism, heresy, political dissension, etc. The opposite claims are also made, albeit by different groups of people.

To make matters more difficult it is clear that in moral, political, cultural, national and similar matters, *we cannot ever expect to get natural unanimity between people and groups of people.*

It might be maintained that people could be brought up and moulded to agree unanimously on important matters of principle. This in fact

[11] This *ratio existendi* is obvious if we think of t he communal structure rather than just the political structure of the group.

might happen. But the unanimity thus produced is not natural and it wasn't found. My argument is that it is less than unlikely that people who were simply appraised of the facts and the tenets of an ideology would unanimously accept it. People react differently when presented with genuinely controversial matters, in fact it is sometimes difficult to convince all of the correctness of non-controversial truths, as is witnessed by the flat earth society.

Thus at the very least before a contrived unanimity is reached, if it can be, we must envisage a period in which there exists an unsatisfactory and possibly unstable system, *made so deliberately* in order to achieve the desired end. This is not satisfactory on non-ideological grounds alone for the endured ills and their consequent communal instability are certain and the future gains hypothetical not to say problematic. Thus the transition period is hard to justify. Another objection can be found in the fact that measures have to be taken to keep unanimity once achieved. These measures will put strains on the system, and inasmuch as these are necessary, the system is inherently unsatisfactory.

In any case as the political scene gets more complex and all-embracing, effective isolation and indoctrination of a population becomes less and less feasible. Thus it becomes progressively less and less reasonable to envisage a system based on contrived unanimity, while natural unanimity is at best only logically possible. Lastly, but not least, where unanimous opinions concerning needs, etc. are enshrined, improvement in terms of real need-satisfaction becomes very much more difficult.

The main argument against basing the system of political control on unanimous opinions of the whole population is that on technical grounds alone it is seen to be inflexible and limited in operation, and taken very strictly it would apply only in very special circumstances if ever. If unanimity once got hold and became the basis of the political system, any change with its possibilities of discord would be dangerous, producing a tendency towards inflexibility detrimental in a changing world. A political system thus based, even if working, would be likely to disallow some real and legitimate needs for it could be argued with transparent plausibility that even if all people were brought up to believe that one and only one style of life is desirable, they would be unlikely to be suited by it *in fact* by reason of different temperaments and nature.

Given lack of unanimity choice between demands becomes necessary, this in turn carries with itself *the difficulty of establishing what reasons are sufficient for interference with people's need and wish satisfaction. This tends to become insoluble if ideological reasons are used in support of the different sides of the argument.* The only solution seems to lie in the banning of ideological considerations, and deciding the cases on other grounds.

To this it might be objected that ideological convictions are among the most important forces that move men, so to disregard them would be to ignore some of the most telling needs, or at the very least, aspirations of men. But then a complete ban is not contemplated. It should be also observed that the acceptance of such ideological demands in their entirety must limit the satisfactoriness of the system severely. Ideological demands even where they do not contain a demand for uniformity *sensu stricto*, are likely to clash without much hope of reconciliation and therefore strife is unavoidable where there is no unanimity. As argued above unanimity is never safe and in the present world almost impossible to achieve, quite apart from the other difficulties mentioned above.

Let us say very generally and with self-conscious oversimplification that every ideological conviction concerns the superiority or desirability of a style of life. Thus one might wish for: Christian, Puritan, Libertarian, Buddhist, Confucian, natural, etc. styles of life. An ideological stand has two facets to it:

(a) There *is the wish* to be able to lead such a desired kind of life, and
(b) There *might be* conjoined to it a demand that others should lead this kind of life as well.[12]

There is some chance of satisfying most people's conviction-bound needs if they were limited only to the first facet, but it is manifestly impossible to satisfy more than one at a time under the second heading given that the prescriptions differ. It is then a reasonable policy to accept ideological convictions under (a) and to strive to provide for the best possible satisfaction of them, and to disregard them under (b).

To adopt this is to opt for a pluralist society where creeds, ideals, convictions, etc. are supposed to co-exist.[13] This goal can be achieved by limiting such "needs" where they interfere with each other and by providing special rules to establish a *modus coexistendi* for differing creeds, ideologies and desires. For example: Rules providing suitable

[12] This is not to be confused with the conviction that this style of life is best for all.

[13] I use the term "pluralist society" in its perhaps old-fashioned sense whereby no more than is indicated here is attributed to a society so named.

areas of liberty for people wishing to practice their convictions; Rules determining ways and means by which communal support or sanction for this, that or another practice can be obtained, and determining the desirable kind of support, etc.

There is at least one style of behaviour that could be desired, and even argued for but that could not be permitted in this kind of society. And this is a creed demanding vicious behaviour incompatible in its very nature with the interests and well-being of others. A murder cult of the Tuareg kind is an example that comes to mind.

It might be objected that societies exist in which vicious and anti-social practices are observed, *viz.* ritual killings, such as child-burnings in ancient Phoenicia, etc. In reply it should be observed that such communities tend to be viable as communities in virtue of those elements of their structure that are unifying rather than in virtue of those that produce strife and insecurity. They tend to be unsatisfactory in virtue of the second class of arrangements. A community's progress can be viewed as going towards fewer and fewer of these and towards smoother and more efficient co-existence and co-operation.

It could be claimed against pluralism that it can be quite inappropriate in certain circumstances. For it would be argued, if there exists a community such that an overwhelming majority of its citizens, even if clearly short of unanimity, share a certain ideological approach, then it is reasonable that they should have the society organized their way.[14]

While a guarded acceptance of some such principle seems reasonable, an argument against it can be produced consisting in the claim that given any person, his claim to organize his own life in his own way, in so far as it does not interfere with others, *is always stronger* than a claim by another person that the first person should organize his life in a way approved of by the other person and unattractive to himself.

Clearly this could be regarded, and defended on moral grounds, but it will suffice to consider it as a basic principle of communal safety. For the adoption of this dictum whilst not hindering any of the needed co-operative and safety measures would nevertheless avoid from the point of view of *every individual* as such, some of the possible ills proceeding from the mere fact that there exist techniques for enforcing co-operation. The ill created by the enforcement of unnecessary cooperation is the frustration and spirit-destroying regimentation of the dissi-

[14] Cf. P. Devlin, *The Enforcement of Morals.* This kind of case would be most favourable to his position, but even this constitutes no argument for ideological uniformity as a principle as applied to other cases.

dent, and the good no more than a feeling of satisfaction or self-righteousness on the part of some others. It will be clear that the good provided is less than the good prevented. Further no one can safely give up this principle unless he is in a position of unchallengeable power; yet those who have such power are precisely those against whom safety measures are needed.

Some further arguments can be provided against the points made in this chapter, but I do not think that they are likely to be fatal. The force of this, that or another consideration might be weakened but the whole line of thought constitutes rather more than just a *prima facie* case for pluralism as here defined. Where a very large majority shows a desire for a certain way of life they should be able to organize the society largely to suit their preference. What commonsense, fairness and safety with regard to dissension and a possible change in the outlook of some or many dictate is this: *Firstly,* there should be a limit to the implementation of the will of the majority, and that comes where others are prevented from leading their lives, especially in private according to their own differing ideas. *Secondly,* provisions should be made for the arrangements to be changed if opinion changes or if some other sufficient reason is demonstrated to obtain. Pluralism need not prevent a community from developing a style of life particularly suitable to its needs as a whole, and to the prevalent convictions of its members, but it is a safeguard against oppressive enforcement of conformity, and provides for flexibility that is a *conditio sine qua non* of survival in a fast changing world.

BIBLIOGRAPHY

A Contribution to the Critique of Political Economy, Preface, K. Marx.

Basic Concepts of Sociology, M. Weber, tr. H. P. Secher, Philosophical Library, N.Y., 1962; Citadel, 1969.

Biological Foundations of Language, E. H. Lenneberg, J. Wiley & Son, N.Y., 1967.

De Regimine Principum, Book I, Ch. I, par. 4, 5, T. Aquinas.

Elementary Forms of Religious Life, E. Durkheim, tr. J. W. Swain, Allen & Unwin, 1915.

Essays in Legal Philosophy, ed. R. S. Summers, Blackwell, 1970.

Ethics and Language, C. L. Stevenson, Yale, 1945.

Fundamental Legal Conceptions as Applied in Judicial Reasoning and Other Legal Essays, W. H. Hohfeld, ed. W. W. Cook, Yale, 1923.

Gesammelte Aufsätze zur Wissenschaftslehre, M. Weber, Mohr, 1922.

Is Law a System of Rules?, R. M. Dworkin, University of Chicago Review, 1967.

K. Marx and F. Engels Selected Correspondence, No. 135 (Marx to Kugelman 1871) K. Marx & F. Engels, Foreign Language Publishing House, Moscow.

Law, Liberty and Morality, H. L. A. Hart, Oxford, 1963.

Leviathan, (1657), T. Hobbes.

"Mill's Liberalism," H. J. McCloskey in *Philosophical Quarterly*, 1963.

"Nature and Convention in a Democratic State," A. B. Gibson in *Australasian Journal of Philosophy*, 1951.

On Civil Government (1689), J. Locke.

Philosophical Investigations, L. Wittgenstein, Blackwell, 1958.

"Philosophy as Strict Science," E. Husserl, tr. Q. Lauer, in *Phenomenology and the Crisis of Philosophy*, Harper & Row, 1965.

Politica – Book I, Ch. 2, Aristotle, tr. Barker, Clarendon Press, 1946.

Political Philosophy, A. Gewirth, Macmillan, 1965.

"Rights," H. J. McCloskey in *Philosophical Quarterly*, 1965.

"Social Justice," A. M. Honore in *McGill Law Journal* 78, 1962.

Social Principles and the Democratic State, S. I. Benn & R. S. Peters, Allen & Unwin, 1959.

The Affluent Society, K. Galbraith, Hamish Hamilton, 1958.

The Concept of Law, H. L. A. Hart, Oxford, 1961.

"The Concept of Truth in Formalised Languages," A. Tarski in *Logic, Semantics, Metamathematics*, Oxford 1956.

The Eighteenth Brumaire of Louis Bonaparte, K. Marx.

The Enforcement of Morals, P. Devlin, Oxford, 1959.

The Idea of Social Science and its Relation to Philosophy, P. Winch, Routledge, 1958.

The Modern Democratic State, A. D. Lindsay, Oxford, 1943.

"The Problem of Liberalism," H. J. McCloskey in *The Review of Metaphysics*, 1965.
The Province of Jurisprudence Determined (1832), J. Austin, ed. H. L. A. Hart, Weidenfeld & Nicholson, London, 1954.
The Social Contract (1762), J. J. Rousseau.
The Spirit of the Laws (1748), Montesquieu.
Word and Object, W. V. O. Quine, MIT Press, 1960.

INDEX